Historical Capitalism
with
Capitalist Civilization

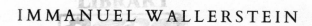

IMMANUEL WALLERSTEIN

V

VERSO

London · New York

© Immanuel Wallerstein 1983
Second Impression 1984
Third Impression 1987
Fourth Impression 1989
Fifth Impression 1992
Sixth Impression 1993
Seventh Impression (new edition incorporating *Capitalist Civilization*) 1995
Eighth Impression 1996

Verso
UK: 6 Meard Street, London W1V 3HR
USA: 180 Varick Street, New York NY 10014–4606

Filmset in Compugraphic Bembo by
Comset Graphic Designs

Printed and bound in Great Britain by
Biddles Ltd, Guildford and King's Lynn

ISBN 1–85984–105–8

Contents

HISTORICAL CAPITALISM

Introduction

This book had its immediate origin in two successive requests. In the autumn of 1980, Thierry Paquot invited me to write a short book for a series he was editing in Paris. He suggested as my topic 'Capitalism'. I replied that I was, in principle, willing to do it, but that I wished my topic to be 'Historical Capitalism'.

I felt that much had been written about capitalism by Marxists and others on the political left, but that most of these books suffered from one of two faults. One variety were basically logico-deductive analyses, starting from definitions of what capitalism was thought to be in essence, and then seeing how far it had developed in various places and times. A second variety concentrated on presumed major transformations of the capitalist system as of some recent point in time, in which the whole earlier point of time served as a mythologized foil against which to treat the empirical reality of the present.

What seemed urgent to me, a task to which in a sense the whole corpus of my recent work has been addressed, was to see capitalism as a historical system, over the whole of its history and in concrete unique reality. I, therefore, set myself the task of describing this reality, of delineating precisely what was always changing and what had not changed at all (such that we could denote the entire reality under one name).

I believe, like many others, that this reality is an integrated whole. But many who assert this view argue it in the form of an attack on others for their alleged 'economism' or their cultural 'idealism' or their over-emphasis on political, 'voluntaristic' factors. Such critiques, almost by their nature, tend to fall by rebound into the sin opposite to the one they are attacking. I have therefore tried to present quite straightforwardly the overall integrated reality, treating successively its expression in the economic, political, and cultural–ideological arenas.

Shortly after I agreed in principle to do this book, I received an invitation from the Department of Political Science at the University of Hawaii to give a series of lectures. I seized the opportunity to write this book as those lectures, given in the spring of 1982. The first version of the first three chapters was presented in Hawaii, and I am grateful to my lively audience for their many comments and criticisms which enabled me to improve the presentation considerably.

One improvement I made was to add the fourth chapter. I realized in the course of the lectures that one problem of exposition persisted: the enormous subterranean strength of the faith in inevitable progress. I realized too that this faith vitiated our understanding of the real historical alternatives before us. I, therefore, decided to address the question directly.

Finally, let me say a word about Karl Marx. He was a monumental figure in modern intellectual and political history. He has bequeathed us a great legacy which is conceptually rich and morally inspiring. When he said, however, that he was not a Marxist, we should take him seriously and not shrug this aside as a *bon mot*.

He knew, as many of his self-proclaimed disciples often do not, that he was a man of the nineteenth century, whose vision was inevitably circumscribed by that social reality. He knew, as many do not, that a theoretical formulation is only understandable and usable in relation to the alternative formulation it is explicitly or implicitly attacking; and that it is entirely irrelevant vis-à-vis formulations about other problems based on other premisses. He knew, as many do not, that there was a tension in the presentation of his work between the exposition of capitalism as a perfected system (which had never in fact existed historically) and the analysis of the concrete day-to-day reality of the capitalist world.

Let us, therefore, use his writings in the only sensible way—that of a comrade in the struggle who knew as much as he knew.

1.
The Commodification of Everything: Production of Capital

Capitalism is first and foremost a historical social system. To understand its origins, its workings, or its current prospects, we have to look at its existing reality. We may of course attempt to summarize that reality in a set of abstract statements, but it would be foolish to use such abstractions to judge and classify the reality. I propose therefore instead to try to describe what capitalism has actually been like in practice, how it has functioned as a system, why it has developed in the ways it has, and where it is presently heading.

The word capitalism is derived from capital. It would be legitimate therefore to presume that capital is a key element in capitalism. But what is capital? In one usage, it is merely accumulated wealth. But when used in the context of historical capitalism it has a more specific definition. It is not just the stock of consumable goods, machinery, or authorized claims to material things in the form of money. Capital in historical capitalism does of course continue to refer to those accumulations of the efforts of past labour which have not yet been expended; but if this were all, then all historical systems back to those of Neanderthal man could be said to have been capitalist, since they all had some such accumulated stocks that incarnated past labour.

What distinguishes the historical social system we are calling historical capitalism is that in this historical system capital came to be used (invested) in a very special way. It came to be used with the primary objective or intent of self-expansion. In this system, past accumulations were 'capital' only to the extend they were used to accumulate more of the same. The process was no doubt complex, even sinuous, as we shall see. But it was this relentless and curiously self-regarding goal of the holder of capital, the accumulation of still more capital, and the relations this holder of capital had therefore to establish with other persons in order to achieve this goal, which we denominate as capitalist. To be sure, this object was not exclusive. Other considerations intruded upon the production process. Still, the question is, in case of conflict, which considerations tended to prevail? Whenever, over time, it was the accumulation of capital that regularly took priority over alternative objectives, we are justified in saying that we are observing a capitalist system in operation.

An individual or a group of individuals might of course decide at any time that they would like to invest capital with the objective of acquiring still more capital. But, before a certain moment in historical time, it had never been easy for such individuals to do this successfully. In previous systems, the long and complex process of the accumulation of capital was almost always blocked at one or another point, even in those cases where its initial condition—the ownership, or amalgamation, of a stock of previously unconsumed goods in the hands of a few—existed. Our putative capitalist always needed to obtain the use of labour, which meant there had to be persons who could be lured or compelled to do such work. Once workers were obtained and goods produced, these goods had to be marketed in some way, which meant there had to be both a system of distribution and a group of buyers with the wherewithal to purchase the goods. The goods had to be sold at a price that was greater than the total costs (as of the point of sale) incurred by the seller, and, furthermore, this margin of difference had to be more than the seller needed for his own subsistence. There had, in our modern language, to be a profit. The owner of the profit then had to be able to retain it until a reasonable opportunity occurred to invest it, whereupon the whole process had to renew itself at the point of production.

In fact, before modern times, this chain of processes (sometimes called the circuit of capital) was seldom completed. For one thing, many of the links in the chain were considered, in previous historical social systems, to be irrational and/or immoral by the holders of political and moral authority. But even in the absence of direct interference by those who had the power to interfere, the process was usually aborted by the non-availability of one or more elements of the process—the accumulated stock in a money form, the labour-power to be utilized by the producer, the network of distributors, the consumers who were purchasers.

One or more elements were missing because, in previous historical social systems, one or more of these elements was not 'commodified' or was insufficiently 'commodified'. What this means is that the process was not considered one that could or should be transacted through a 'market'. Historical capitalism involved therefore the widespread commodification of processes—not merely exchange processes, but production processes, distribution processes, and investment processes—that had previously been conducted other than via a 'market'. And, in the course of seeking to accumulate more and more capital, capitalists have sought to commodify more and more of these social processes in all spheres of economic life. Since capitalism is a self-regarding process, it follows that no social transaction has been intrinsically exempt from possible inclusion. That is why we may say that the historical development of capitalism has involved the thrust towards the commodification of everything.

Nor has it been enough to commodify the social processes. Production processes were linked to one another in complex commodity chains. For example, consider a typical product that has been widely produced and sold throughout the historical experience of capitalism, an item of clothing. To produce an item of clothing, one typically needs at the very least cloth, thread, some kind of machinery, and labour-power. But each of these items in turn has to be produced. And the items that go into their production in turn have also to be produced. It was not inevitable—it was not even common—that every subprocess in this commodity chain was commodified. Indeed, as we shall see, profit is often greater when not all links in the chain are in fact commodified. What is clear is that, in such a chain, there is a very large and dispersed set of workers who are receiving some sort of remuneration which registers on the balance-sheet as costs. There is also a far smaller, but also usually dispersed, set of persons (who are furthermore usually not united as economic partners but operate as distinct economic entities), who share in some way in the ultimate margin that exists in the commodity chain between the total costs of production of the chain and the total income realized by the disposal of the final product.

Once there were such commodity chains linking multiple production processes, it is clear that the rate of accumulation for all the 'capitalists' put together became a function of how wide a margin could be created, in a situation where this margin could fluctuate considerably. The rate of accumulation for particular capitalists, however, was a function of a process of 'competition', with higher rewards going to those who had greater perspicacity of judgement, greater ability to control their work-force, and greater access to politically-decided constraints on particular market operations (known generically as 'monopolies').

This created a first elementary contradiction in the system. While the interest of all capitalists, taken as a class, seemed to be to reduce all costs of production, these reductions in fact frequently favoured particular capitalists against others, and some therefore preferred to increased their share of a smaller global margin rather than accept a smaller share of a larger global margin. Futhermore, there was a second fundamental contradiction in the system. As more and more capital was accumulated, more and more processes commodified, and more and more commodities produced, one of the key requirements to maintain the flow was that there be more and more purchasers. However, at the same time, efforts to reduce the costs of production often reduced the flow and distribution of money, and thus inhibited the steady expansion of purchasers, needed to complete the process of accumulation. On the other hand, redistributions of global profit in ways that could have expanded the network of purchasers often reduced the global margin of profit. Hence individual entrepreneurs found themselves pushing in one direction for their own enterprises (for example, by reducing their own labour costs), while simultaneously pushing (as members of a collective class) to increase the overall network of purchasers (which inevitably involved, for some producers at least, an increase in labour costs).

The economics of capitalism has thus been governed by the rational intent to maximize accumulation. But what was rational for the entrepreneurs was not necessarily rational for the workers. And even more important, what was rational for all entrepreneurs as a collective group was not necessarily rational for any given entrepreneur. It is therefore not enough to say that everyone was pursuing their own interests. Each person's own interests often pushed them, quite 'rationally', to engage in contradictory activities. The calculation of real long-term interest thereby became exceedingly complex, even if we ignore, at present, the degree to which everyone's perceptions of their own interests was clouded over and distorted by complex ideological veils. For the moment, I provisionally assume that historical capitalism did in fact breed a *homo economicus*, but I am adding that he was almost inevitably a bit confused.

This is however one 'objective' constraint which limited the confusion. If a given individual constantly made errors in economic judgement, whether because of ignorance, fatuity, or ideological prejudice, this individual (firm) tended not to survive in the market. Bankruptcy has been the harsh cleansing fluid of the capitalist system, constantly forcing all economic actors to keep more or less to the well-trodden rut, pressuring them to act in such a way that collectively there has been even further accumulation of capital.

Historical capitalism, is, thus, that concrete, time-bounded, space-bounded integrated locus of productive activities within which the endless accumulation of capital has been the economic objective or 'law' that has governed or prevailed in fundamental economic activity. It is that social system in which those who have operated by such rules have had such great impact on the whole as to create conditions wherein the others have been forced to conform to the patterns or to suffer the consequences. It is that social system in which the scope of these rules (the law of value) has grown ever wider, the enforcers of these rules ever more intransigent, the penetration of these rules into the social fabric ever greater, even while social opposition to these rules has grown ever louder and more organized.

Using this description of what one means by historical capitalism, each of us can determine to which concrete, time-bounded, space-bounded integrated locus this refers. My own view is that the genesis of this historical system is located in late-fifteenth-century Europe, that the system expanded in space over time to cover the entire globe by the late nineteenth century, and that it still today covers the entire globe. I realize that such a cursory delineation of the time-space boundaries evokes doubts in many minds. These doubts are however of two different kinds. First, empirical doubts. Was Russia inside or outside the European world-economy in the sixteenth century? Exactly when was the Ottoman Empire incorporated into the capitalist world-system? Can we consider a given interior zone of a given state at a given time as truly 'integrated' into the capitalist world-economy? These questions are important, both in themselves, and because in attempting to answer them we are forced to make more precise our analyses of the processes of historical capitalism. But this is neither the moment nor place to address these numerous empirical queries that are under continuing debate and elaboration.

The second kind of doubt is that which addresses the very utility of the inductive classification I have just suggested. There are those who refuse to accept that capitalism can ever be said to exist unless there is a specific form of social relation in the workplace, that of a private entrepreneur employing wage-labourers. There are those who wish to say that when a given state has nationalized its industries and proclaimed its allegiance to socialist doctrines, it has, by those acts and as a result of their consequences, ended the participation of that state in the capitalist world-system. These are not empirical queries but theoretical ones, and we shall try to address them in the course of this discussion. Addressing them deductively would be pointless however as it would lead not to a rational debate, but merely to a clash of opposing faiths. We shall therefore address them heuristically, arguing that our inductive classification is more useful than alternative ones, because it comprehends more easily and elegantly what we collectively know at present about historical reality, and because it affords us an interpretation of this reality which enables us to act more efficaciously on the present.

Let us therefore look at how the capitalist system actually has functioned. To say that a producer's objective is the accumulation of capital is to say that he will seek to produce as much of a given good as possible and offer it for sale at the highest profit margin to him. He will do this however within a series of economic constraints which exist, as we say, 'in the market'. His total production is perforce limited by the (relatively immediate) availability of such things as material inputs, a work-force, customers, and access to cash to expand his investment base. The amount he can profitably produce and the profit margin he can claim is also limited by the ability of his 'competitors' to offer the same item at lower sales prices; not in this case competitors anywhere in the world market, but those located in the same immediate, more circumscribed local markets in which he actually sells (however this market be defined in a given instance). The expansion of his production will also be constrained by the degree to which his expanded production will create such a price-reducing effect in the 'local' market as to actually reduce the real total profit realized on his total production.

These are all objective constraints, meaning they exist in the absence of any particular set of decisions by a given producer or by others active in the market. These constraints are the consequence of the total social process that exists in a concrete time and place. There are always in addition of course other constraints, more open to manipulation. Governments may adopt, may already have adopted, various rules which in some way transform economic options and therefore the calculus of profit. A given producer may be the beneficiary or the victim of existing rules. A given producer may seek to persuade political authorities to change their rules in his favour.

How have producers operated so as to maximize their ability to accumulate capital? Labour-power has always been a central and quantitatively significant element in the production-process. The producer seeking to accumulate is concerned with two different aspects of labour-power: its availability and its cost. The problem of availability has usually been posed in the following manner: social relations of production that were fixed (a stable work-force for a given producer) might be low-cost if the market were stable and the size of his work-force optimal for a given time. But if the market for the product declined, the fact that the work-force was fixed would increase its real cost for the producer. And should the market for the product increase, the fact that the work-force was fixed would make it impossible for the producer to take advantage of the profit opportunities.

On the other hand, variable work-forces also had disadvantages for the capitalists. Variable work-forces were by definition work-forces that were not necessarily continuously working for the same producer. Such workers must therefore, in terms of survival, have been concerned with their rate of remuneration in terms of a time-span long enough to level out variations in real income. That is, workers had to be able to make enough from the employment to cover periods when they did not receive remuneration. Consequently, variable work-forces often cost producers more per hour per individual than fixed work-forces.

When we have a contradiction, and we have one here in the very heart of the capitalist production process, we can be sure that the result will be a historically uneasy compromise. Let us review what in fact happened. In historical systems preceding historical capitalism, most (never all) work-forces were fixed. In some cases, the producer's work-force was only himself or his family, hence by definition fixed. In some cases, a non kin-related work-force was bonded to a particular producer through various legal and/or customary regulations (including various forms of slavery, debt bondage, serfdom, permanent tenancy arrangements, etc.). Sometimes the bonding was life-time. Sometimes it was for limited periods, with an option of renewal; but such time-limitation was only meaningful if realistic alternatives existed at the moment of renewal. Now the fixity of these arrangements posed problems not only for the particular producers to whom a given work-force was bonded. It posed problems to all other producers as well, since obviously other producers could only expand their activities to the extent that there existed available, non-fixed work-forces.

These considerations formed the basis, as has so often been described, of the rise of the institution of wage-labour, where-in a group of persons existed who were permanently available for employment, more or less to the highest bidder. We refer to this process as the operation of a labour market, and to the persons who sell their labour as proletarians. I do not tell you anything novel to say that, in historical capitalism, there has been increasing proletarianization of the work-force. The statement is not only not novel; it is not in the least sur-prising. The advantages to producers of the process of proletarianization have been amply documented. What is surprising is not that there has been so much proletarianization, but that there has been so little. Four hundred years at least into the existence of a historical social system, the amount of fully proletarianized labour in the capitalist world-economy today cannot be said to total even fifty per cent.

To be sure this statistic is a function of how you measure it and whom you are measuring. If we use official government statistics on the so-called economically active labour-force, primarily adult males who make themselves formally available for remunerated labour, we may find that the percentage of wage-workers is said today to be reasonably high (although even then, when calculated world-wide, the actual percentage is smaller than most theoretical statements presume). If however we consider all persons whose work is incorporated in one way or another into the commodity chains—thus embracing virtually all adult women, and a very large proportion of persons at the pre-adult and post-prime adulthood age range (that is, the young and the old) as well—then our percentage of proletarians drastically drops.

Let us furthermore take one additional step before we do our measuring. Is it conceptually useful to apply the label 'proletarian' to an individual? I doubt it. Under historical capitalism, as under previous historical systems, individuals have tended to live their lives within the framework of relatively stable structures which share a common fund of current income and accumulated capital, which we may call households. The fact that the boundaries of these households are constantly changing by the entries and exits of individuals does not make these households less the unit of rational calculation in terms of remuneration and expenditure. People who wish to survive count all their potential income, from no matter what source, and assess it in terms of the real expenditures they must make. They seek minimally to survive; then with more income, to enjoy a life-style which they find satisfying; and ultimately, with still more, to enter the capitalist game as accumulators of capital. For all real purposes, it is the household that has been the economic unit that has engaged in these activities. This household has usually been a kin-related unit, but sometimes not or, at least, not exclusively. This household has for the most part been co-residential, but less so as commodification proceeded.

It is in the context of such a household structure that a social distinction between productive and unproductive work began to be imposed on the working classes. De facto, productive work came to be defined as money-earning work (primarily wage-earning work), and non-productive work as work that, albeit very necessary, was merely 'subsistence' activity and therefore was said to produce no 'surplus' which anyone else could possibly appropriate. This work was either totally non-commodified or involved petty (but then truly petty) commodity production. The differentiation between kinds of work was anchored by creating specific roles attached to them. Productive (wage) labour became the task primarily of the adult male/father and secondarily of other (younger) adult males in the household. Non-productive (subsistence) labour became the task primarily of the adult female/mother and secondarily of other females, plus the children and the elderly. Productive labour was done outside the household in the 'work place'. Non-productive labour was done inside the household.

The lines of division were not absolute, to be sure, but they became under historical capitalism quite clear and compelling.

A division of real labour by gender and age was not of course an invention of historical capitalism. It has probably always existed, if only because for some tasks there are biological prerequisites and limitations (of gender, but also of age). Nor was a hierarchical family and/or household structure an invention of capitalism. That too had long existed.

What was new under historical capitalism was the correlation of division of labour and valuation of work. Men may often have done different work from women (and adults different work from children and the elderly), but under historical capitalism there has been a steady devaluation of the work of women (and of the young and old), and a corresponding emphasis on the value of the adult male's work. Whereas in other systems men and women did specified (but normally equal) tasks, under historical capitalism the adult male wage-earner was classified as the 'breadwinner', and the adult female home-worker as the 'housewife.' Thus when national statistics began to be compiled, itself a product of a capitalist system, all breadwinners were considered members of the economically active labour-force, but no housewives were. Thus was sexism institutionalized. The legal and paralegal apparatus of gender distinction and discrimination followed quite logically in the wake of this basic differential valuation of labour.

We may note here that the concepts of extended childhood/adolescence and of a 'retirement' from the work-force not linked to illness or frailty have been also specific concomitants of the emerging household structures of historical capitalism. They have often been viewed as 'progressive' exemptions from work. They may however be more accurately viewed as redefinitions of work as non-work. Insult has been added to injury by labelling children's training activities and the miscellaneous tasks of retired adults as somehow 'fun', and the devaluation of their work contributions as the reasonable counterpart of their release from the 'drudgery' of 'real' work.

As an ideology, these distinctions helped ensure that the commodification of labour was extensive but at the same time limited. For example, if we were to calculate how many households in the world-economy have obtained more than fifty per cent of their real income (or total revenue in all forms) from wage-work outside the household, I think we would be quickly amazed by the lowness of the percentage; this is the case not only in earlier centuries but even today, although the percentage has probably been steadily growing over the historical development of the capitalist world-economy.

How can we account for this? I don't think it's very difficult. On the assumption that a producer employing wage-labour would prefer to pay less rather than more, always and everywhere, the lowness of the level at which wage-workers could afford to accept employment has been a function of the kind of households in which the wage-workers have been located throughout their life-spans. Put very simply, for identical work at identical levels of efficiency, the wage-worker located in a household with a high percentage of wage income (let us call this a proletarian household) had had a higher monetary threshold below which he would have found it manifestly irrational for him to do wage work than a wage-worker located in a household that has a low percentage of wage income (let us call this a semi-proletarian household).

The reason for this difference of what we might call the minimum-acceptable-wage threshold has to do with the economics of survival. Where a proletarian household depended primarily upon wage-income, then that had to cover the minimal costs of survival and reproduction. However, when wages formed a less important segment of total household income, it would often be rational for an individual to accept employment at a rate of remuneration which contributed less than its proportionate share (in terms of hours worked) of real income—whilst nevertheless resulting in the earning of necessary liquid cash (the necessity frequently being legally imposed)—or else involved the substitution of this wage-remunerated work for labour in still less remunerative tasks.

What happened then in such semi-proletarian households is that those who were producing other forms of real income—that is, basically household production for self-consumption, or sale in a local market, or of course both—whether these were other persons in the household (of any sex or age) or the same person at other moments of his life-span, were creating surpluses which lowered the minimum-acceptable-wage threshold. In this way, non-wage work permitted some producers to remunerate their work-force at lower rates, thereby reducing their cost of production and increasing their profit margins. No wonder then, as a general rule, that any employer of wage-labour would prefer to have his wage-workers located in semi-proletarian rather than in proletarian households. If we now look at global empirical reality throughout the time-space of historical capitalism, we suddenly discover that the location of wage-workers in semi-proletarian rather than in proletarian households has been the statistical norm. Intellectually, our problem suddenly gets turned upside down. From explaining the reasons for the existence of proletarianization, we have moved to explaining why the process was so incomplete. We now have to go even further—

why has proletarianization proceeded at all?

Let me say immediately that it is very doubtful that increasing world proletarianization can be attributed primarily to the socio-political pressures of entrepreneurial strata. Quite the contrary. It would seem they have had many motives to drag their feet. First of all, as we have just argued, the transformation of a significant number of semi-proletarian households into proletarian households in a given zone tended to raise the real minimum-wage-level, paid by the employers of wage-labour. Secondly, increased proletarianization had political consequences, as we shall discuss later, which were both negative for the employers and also cumulative, thereby eventually increasing still further the levels of wage-payments in given geographico-economic zones. Indeed, so much were employers of wage-labour unenthusiastic about proletarianization that, in addition to fostering the gender/age division of labour, they also encouraged, in their employment patterns and through their influence in the political arena, recognition of defined ethnic groups, seeking to link them to specific allocated roles in the labour-force, with different levels of real remuneration for their work. Ethnicity created a cultural crust which consolidated the patterns of semi-proletarian household structures. That the emergence of such ethnicity also played a politically-divisive role for the working classes has been a political bonus for the employers but not, I think, the prime mover in this process.

Before however we can understand how there has come to be any increase at all in proletarianization over time in historical capitalism, we have to return to the issue of the commodity chains in which the multiple specific production activities are located. We must rid ourselves of the simplistic image that the 'market' is a place where initial producer and ultimate consumer meet. No doubt there are and always have been such market-places. But in historical capitalism, such market-place transactions have constituted a small percentage of the whole. Most transactions have involved exchange between two intermediate producers located on a long commodity chain. The purchaser was purchasing an 'input' for his production process. The seller was selling a 'semi-finished product', semi-finished that is in terms of its ultimate use in direct individual consumption.

The struggle over price in these 'intermediate markets' represented an effort by the buyer to wrest from the seller a proportion of the profit realized from all prior labour processes throughout the commodity chain. This struggle to be sure was determined at particular space-time nexuses by supply and demand, but never uniquely. In the first place, of course, supply and demand can be manipulated through monopolistic constraints, which have been commonplace rather than exceptional. Secondly, the seller can affect the price at the nexus through vertical integration. Whenever the 'seller' and the 'buyer' were in fact ultimately the same firm, the price could be arbitrarily juggled in terms of fiscal and other considerations, but such a price never represented the interplay of supply and demand. Vertical integration, just like the 'horizontal' monopoly, has not been rare. We are of course familiar with its most spectacular instances: the chartered companies of the sixteenth to eighteenth centuries, the great merchant houses of the nineteenth, the transnational corporations of the twentieth. These were global structures seeking to encompass as many links in a particular commodity chain as possible. But smaller instances of vertical integration, covering only a few (even two) links in a chain, have been even more widespread. It seems reasonable to argue that vertical integration has been the statistical norm of historical capitalism rather than those 'market' nexuses in commodity chains in which seller and buyer were truly distinct and antagonistic.

Now commodity chains have not been random in their geographical directions. Were they all plotted on maps, we would notice that they have been centripetal in form. Their points of origin have been manifold, but their points of destination have tended to converge in a few areas. That is to say, they have tended to move from the peripheries of the capitalist world-economy to the centres or cores. It is hard to contest this as an empirical observation. The real question is why this has been so. To talk of commodity chains means to talk of an extended social division of labour which, in the course of capitalism's historical development, has become more and more functionally and geographically extensive, and simultaneously more and more hierarchical. This hierarchization of space in the structure of productive processes has led to an ever greater polarization between the core and peripheral zones of the world-economy, not only in terms of distributive criteria (real income levels, quality of life) but even more importantly in the loci of the accumulation of capital.

Initially, as this process began, the spatial differentials were rather small, and the degree of spatial specialization limited. Within the capitalist system, however, whatever differentials existed (whether for ecological or historical reasons) were exaggerated, reinforced, and encrusted. What was crucial in this process was the intrusion of force into the determination of price. To be sure, the use of force by one party in a market transaction in order to improve his price was no invention of capitalism. Unequal exchange is an ancient practice. What was remarkable about capitalism as a historical system was the way in which this unequal exchange could be hidden; indeed, hidden so well that it is only after five hundred years of the operation of this mechanism that even the avowed opponents of the system have begun to unveil it systematically.

The key to hiding this central mechanism lay in the very structure of the capitalist world-economy, the seeming separation in the capitalist world-system of the economic arena (a world-wide social division of labour with integrated production processes all operating for the endless accumulation of capital) and the political arena (consisting ostensibly of separate sovereign states, each with autonomous responsibility for political decisions within its jurisdiction, and each disposing of armed forces to sustain its authority). In the real world of historical capitalism, almost all commodity chains of any importance have traversed these state frontiers. This is not a recent innovation. It has been true from the very beginning of historical capitalism. Moreover, the transnationality of commodity chains is as descriptively true of the sixteenth-century capitalist world as of the twentieth-century.

How did this unequal exchange work? Starting with any real differential in the market, occurring because of either the (temporary) scarcity of a complex production process, or artificial scarcities created *manu militari*, commodities moved between zones in such a way that the area with the less 'scarce' item 'sold' its items to the other area at a price that incarnated more real input (cost) than an equally-priced item moving in the opposite direction. What really happened is that there was a transfer of part of the total profit (or surplus) being produced from one zone to another. Such a relationship is that of coreness-peripherality. By extension, we can call the losing zone a 'periphery' and the gaining zone a 'core'. These names in fact reflect the geographical structure of the economic flows.

We find immediately several mechanisms that historically have increased the disparity. Whenever a 'vertical integration' of any two links on a commodity chain occurred, it was possible to shift an even larger segment of the total surplus towards the core than had previously been possible. Also, the shift of surplus towards the core concentrated capital there and made available disproportionate funds for further mechanization, both allowing producers in core zones to gain additional competitive advantages in existing products and permitting them to create ever new rare products with which to renew the process.

The concentration of capital in core zones created both the fiscal base and the political motivation to create relatively strong state-machineries, among whose many capacities was that of ensuring that the state machineries of peripheral zones became or remained relatively weaker. They could thereby pressure these state-structures to accept, even promote, greater specialization in their jurisdiction in tasks lower down the hierarchy of commodity chains, utilizing lower-paid work-forces and creating (reinforcing) the relevant household structures to permit such work-forces to survive. Thus did historical capitalism actually create the so-called historical levels of wages which have become so dramatically divergent in different zones of the world-system.

We say this process is hidden. By that we mean that actual prices always seemed to be negotiated in a world market on the basis of impersonal economic forces. The enormous apparatus of latent force (openly used sporadically in wars and

colonization) has not had to be invoked in each separate transaction to ensure that the exchange was unequal. Rather, the
apparatus of force came into play only when there were significant challenges to an existing level of unequal exchange.
Once the acute political conflict was past, the world's entrepreneurial classes could pretend that the economy was operating solely by considerations of supply and demand, without
acknowledging how the world-economy had historically ar-
rived at a particular point of supply and demand, and what
structures of force were sustaining at that very moment the
'customary' differentials in levels of wages and of the real
quality of life of the world's work-forces.

We may now return to the question of why there has been
any proletarianization at all. Let us remember the fundamental
contradiction between the individual interest of each entrepreneur and the collective interest of all capitalist classes. Unequal exchange by definition served these collective interests
but not many individual interests. It follows that those whose
interests were not immediately served at any given time (because they gained less than their competitors) constantly tried
to alter things in their favour. They tried, that is, to compete
more successfully in the market, either by making their own
production more efficient, or by using political influence to
create a new monopolistic advantage for themselves.

Acute competition among capitalists has always been one of
the *differentia specifica* of historical capitalism. Even when it
seemed to be voluntarily restrained (by cartel-like arrangements), this was primarily because each competitor thought
that such restraint optimized his own margins. In a system
predicated on the endless accumulation of capital, no partici-
pant could afford to drop this enduring thrust towards long-

run profitability except at the risk of self-destruction.

Thus monopolistic practice and competitive motivation have been a paired reality of historical capitalism. In such circumstances, it is evident that no specific pattern linking the productive processes could be stable. Quite the contrary: it would always be in the interests of a large number of competing entrepreneurs to try to alter the specific pattern of given time-places without short-term concern for the global impact of such behaviour. Adam Smith's 'unseen hand' unquestionably operated, in the sense that the 'market' set constraints on individual behaviour, but it would be a very curious reading of historical capitalism that suggested that the outcome has been harmony.

Rather, the outcome has seemed, once again as an empirical observation, to be an alternating cycle of expansions and stagnations in the system as a whole. These cycles have involved fluctuations of such significance and regularity that it is hard not to believe that they are intrinsic to the workings of the system. They seem, if the analogy be permitted, to be the breathing mechanism of the capitalist organism, inhaling the purifying oxygen and exhaling poisonous waste. Analogies are always dangerous but this one seems particularly apt. The wastes that accumulated were the economic inefficiencies that recurrently got politically encrusted through the process of unequal exchange described above. The purifying oxygen was the more efficient allocation of resources (more efficient in terms of permitting further accumulation of capital) which the regular restructuring of the commodity chains permitted.

What seems to have happened every fifty years or so is that in the efforts of more and more entrepreneurs to gain for themselves the more profitable nexuses of commodity chains, disproportions of investment occurred such that we speak, somewhat misleadingly, of overproduction. The only solution to these disproportions has been a shakedown of the productive system, resulting in a more even distribution. This sounds logical and simple, but its fall-out has always been massive. It has meant each time further concentration of operations in those links in the commodity chains which have been most clogged. This has involved the elimination of both some entrepreneurs and some workers (those who worked for entrepreneurs who went out of business and also those who worked for others who further mechanized in order to reduce the costs of unit production). Such a shift also enabled entrepreneurs to 'demote' operations in the hierarchy of the commodity chain, thereby enabling them to devote investment funds and effort to innovative links in the commodity chains which, because initially offering 'scarcer' inputs, were more profitable. 'Demotion' of particular processes on the hierarchical scale also often led to geographical relocation in part. Such geographical relocation found a major attraction in the move to a lower labour-cost area, though from the point of view of the area into which the industry has moved the new industry usually involved an increase in the wage-level for some segments of the work-force. We are living through precisely such a massive world-wide relocation right now of the world's automobile, steel, and electronics industries. This phenomenon of relocation has been part and parcel of historical capitalism from the outset.

There have been three major consequences of these reshuffles. One is the constant geographical restructuring itself of the capitalist world-system. Nonetheless, although commodity chains have been significantly restructured every fifty years or so, a system of hierarchically-organized commodity chains has been retained. Particular production processes have moved down the hierarchy, as new ones are inserted at the top. And particular geographic zones have housed ever-shifting hierarchical levels of processes. Thus, given products have had 'product cycles', starting off as core products and eventually becoming peripheral products. Furthermore, given loci have moved up or down, in terms of comparative well-being of their inhabitants. But to call such reshuffles 'development', we would first have to demonstrate a reduction of the global polarization of the system. Empirically, this simply does not seem to have happened; rather polarization has historically increased. These geographical and product relocations then may be said to have been truly cyclical.

However, there was a second, quite different consequence of the reshufflings. Our misleading word, 'overproduction', does call attention to the fact that the immediate dilemma has always operated through the absence of sufficient worldwide effective demand for some key products of the system. It is in this situation that the interests of the work-forces coincided with the interests of a minority of entrepreneurs. Work-forces have always sought to increase their share of the surplus, and moments of economic breakdown of the system have often provided both extra immediate incentive and some extra opportunity to pursue their class struggles. One of the most effective and immediate ways for work-forces to increase real income has been the further commodification of their own labour. They have often sought to substitute wage-labour for those parts of the household production processes which have brought in low amounts of real income, in particular for various kinds of petty commodity production. One of the major forces behind proletarianization has been the world's work-forces themselves. They have understood, often better than their self-proclaimed intellectual spokesmen, how much greater the exploitation is in semi-proletarian than in more fully-proletarianized households.

It is at moments of stagnation that some owner-producers, in part responding to political pressure from the work-forces, in part believing that structural changes in the relations of production would benefit them vis-à-vis competing owner producers, have joined forces, both in the production and political arenas, to push for the further proletarianization of a limited segment of the work-force, somewhere. It is this process which gives us the major clue as to why there has been any increase in proletarianization at all, given that proletarianization has in the long term led to reduced profit levels in the capitalist world-economy.

It is in this context that we should consider the process of technological change which has been less the motor than the consequence of historical capitalism. Each major technological 'innovation' has been primarily the creation of new 'scarce' products, as such highly profitable, and secondarily of labour-reducing processes. They were responses to the downturns in the cycles, ways of appropriating the 'inventions' to further the process of capital accumulation. These innovations no doubt frequently affected the actual organization of production. They pushed historically towards the centralization of many work processes (the factory, the assembly line). But it is easy to exaggerate how much change there has been. Processes of concentration of physical production tasks have frequently been investigated without regard to counteracting decentralization processes.

This is especially true if we put into the picture the third consequence of the cyclical reshuffling. Notice that, given the two consequences already mentioned, we have a seeming paradox to explain. On the one hand, we spoke of the continuous concentration of capital accumulation in historical polarization of distribution. Simultaneously, however, we spoke of a slow, but nonetheless steady, process of proletarianization which, we argued, actually has reduced profit levels. One easy resolution would be to say the first process is simply greater than the second, which is true. But in addition the decrease in profit levels occasioned by increased proletarianization has hitherto been more than compensated by a further mechanism moving in the opposite direction.

Another easy empirical observation to make about historical capitalism is that its geographical situs has grown steadily larger over time. Once again, the pace of the process offers the best clue to its explanation. The incorporation of new zones into the social division of labour of historical capitalism did not occur all at once. It in fact occurred in periodic spurts, although each successive expansion seemed to be limited in scope. Undoubtedly part of the explanation lies in the very technological development of historical capitalism itself. Improvements in transport, communications, and armaments made it steadily less expensive to incorporate regions further and further from the core zones. But this explanation at best gives us a necessary but not sufficient condition for the process.

It has sometimes been asserted that the explanation lies in the constant search for new markets in which to realize the profits of capitalist production. This explanation however simply does not accord with the historical facts. Areas external to historical capitalism have on the whole been reluctant purchasers of its products, in part because they didn't 'need' them in terms of their own economic system and in part because they often lacked the relevant wherewithal to purchase them. To be sure there were exceptions. But by and large it was the capitalist world that sought out the products of the external arena and not the other way around. Whenever particular loci were militarily conquered, capitalist entrepreneurs regularly complained of the absence of real markets there and operated through colonial governments to 'create tastes'. The search for markets as an explanation simply does not hold. A much more plausible explanation is the search for low-cost labour forces. It is historically the case that virtually every new zone incorporated into the world-economy established levels of real remuneration which were at the bottom of the world-system's hierarchy of wage-levels. They had virtually no fully proletarian households and were not at all encouraged to develop them. On the contrary, the policies of the colonial states (and of the restructured semi-colonial states in those incorporated zones that were not formally colonized) seemed designed precisely to promote the emergence of the very semi-proletarian household which, as we have seen, made possible the lowest possible wage-level threshold. Typical state policies involved combining taxation mechanisms, which forced every household to engage in some wage-labour, with restrictions on movement or forced separation of household members, which reduced considerably the possibility of full proletarianization.

If we add to this analysis the observation that new incorporations into the world-system of capitalism tended to correlate with phases of stagnation in the world-economy, it becomes clear that geographical expansion of the world-system served to counterbalance the profit-reducing process of increased proletarianization, by incorporating new workforces destined to be semi-proletarianized. The seeming paradox has disappeared. The impact of proletarianization on the process of polarization has been matched, perhaps more

than matched, at least hitherto, by the impact of incorporations. And factory-like work processes as a percentage of the
whole have expanded less than is usually asserted, given the
steadily expanding denominator of the equation.

We have spent much time on delineating how historical
capitalism has operated in the narrowly economic arena. We
are now ready to explain why capitalism emerged as a historical social system. This is not as easy as is often thought. On
the face of it, far from being a 'natural' system, as some apol-
ogists have tried to argue, historical capitalism is a patently absurd one. One accumulates capital in order to accumulate
more capital. Capitalists are like white mice on a treadmill,
running ever faster in order to run still faster. In the process,
no doubt, some people live well, but others live miserably;
and how well, and for how long, do those who live well live?

The more I have reflected upon it the more absurd it has
seemed to me. Not only do I believe that the vast majority of
the populations of the world are objectively and subjectively
less well-off materially than in previous historical systems but,
as we shall see, I think it can be argued that they have been
politically less well off also. So imbued are we all by the self-
justifying ideology of progress which this historical system has
fashioned, that we find it difficult even to recognize the vast
historical negatives of this system. Even so stalwart a de-
nouncer of historical capitalism as Karl Marx laid great emphasis on its historically progressive role. I do not believe this
at all, unless by 'progressive' one simply means that which is
historically later and whose origins can be explained by something that preceded it. The balance-sheet of historical capitalism, to which I shall return, is perhaps complex, but the initial calculus in terms of material distribution of goods and
allocation of energies is in my view very negative indeed.

If this is so, why did such a system arise? Perhaps, precisely to achieve this end. What could be more plausible than a line of reasoning which argues that the explanation of the origin of a system was to achieve an end that has in fact been achieved? I know that modern science has turned us from the search for final causes and from all considerations of intentionality (especially since they are so inherently difficult to demonstrate empirically). But modern science and historical capitalism have been in close alliance as we know; thus, we must suspect the authority of science on precisely this question: the modality of knowing the origins of modern capitalism. Let me therefore simply outline a historical explanation of the origins of historical capitalism without attempting to develop here the empirical base for such an argument.

In the world of the fourteenth and fifteenth centuries, Europe was the locus of a social division of labour which, in comparison with other areas of the world, was, in terms of the forces of production, the cohesion of its historical system, and its relative state of human knowledge, an in-between zone— neither as advanced as some areas nor as primitive as others. Marco Polo, we must remember, coming from one of the most culturally and economically 'advanced' subregions of Europe, was quite overwhelmed with what he encountered on his Asian voyages.

The economic arena of feudal Europe was going through a very fundamental, internally generated, crisis in this period that was shaking its social foundations. Its ruling classes were destroying each other at a great rate, while its land-system (the basis of its economic structure) was coming loose, with considerable reorganization moving in the direction of a far more egalitarian distribution than had been the norm. Furthermore, small peasant farmers were demonstrating great efficiency as producers. The political structures were in general getting weaker and their preoccupation with the internecine struggles of the politically powerful meant that little time was left for repressing the growing strength of the masses of the population. The ideological cement of Catholicism was under great strain and egalitarian movements were being born in the very bosom of the Church. Things were indeed falling apart. Had Europe continued on the path along which it was going, it is difficult to believe that the patterns of medieval feudal Europe with its highly structured system of 'orders' could have been reconsolidated. Far more probable is that the European feudal social structure would have evolved towards a system of relatively equal small-scale producers, further flattening out the aristocracies and decentralizing the political structures.

Whether this would have been good or bad, and for whom, is a matter of speculation and of little interest. But it is clear that the prospect must have appalled Europe's upper strata—appalled and frightened them, especially as they felt their ideological armour was disintegrating too. Without suggesting that anyone consciously verbalized any such attempt, we can see by comparing the Europe of 1650 with 1450 that the following things had occurred. By 1650, the basic structures of historical capitalism as a viable social system had been established and consolidated. The trend towards egalitarianization of reward had been drastically reversed. The upper strata were once again in firm control politically and ideologically. There was a reasonably high level of continuity between the families that had been high strata in 1450 and those that were high strata in 1650. Furthermore, if one substituted 1900 for 1650, one would find that most of the comparisons with 1450 still hold true. It is only in the twentieth century that there are some significant trends in a different direction, a sign as we shall see that the historical system of capitalism has, after four to five hundred years of flourishing, finally come into structural crisis.

No one may have verbalized the intent, but it certainly seems to have been the case that the creation of historical capitalism as a social system dramatically reversed a trend that the upper strata feared, and established in its place one that served their interests even better. Is that so absurd? Only to those who were its victims.

2.
The Politics
of Accumulation:
Struggle for Benefits

The endless accumulation of capital for its own sake may seem *prima facie* to be a socially absurd objective. It has had however its defenders, who usually justified it by the long-term social benefits in which it purported to result. We shall discuss later the degree to which these social benefits are real. Quite aside however from any collective benefits it is clear that the amassing of capital affords the opportunity and the occasion for much increased consumption by many individuals (and/or small groups). Whether increased consumption actually improves the quality of life of the consumers is another question and one we shall also postpone.

The first question we shall address is: who gets the immediate individual benefits? It seems reasonable to assert that most people have not waited upon evaluations of *long-term* benefits or the quality of life resulting from such consumption (either for the collectivity or for the individuals) to decide that it is worthwhile to struggle for the immediate individual benefits that were so obviously available. Indeed this has been the central focus of political struggle within historical capitalism. This is in fact what we mean when we say that historical capitalism is a materialist civilization.

In material terms, not only have the rewards been great to those who have come out ahead, but the differentials in material rewards between the top and the bottom have been great and growing greater over time in the world-system taken as a whole. We have already discussed the economic processes that accounted for this polarization of distribution of reward. We should now turn our attention to how people have manoeuvred within such an economic system to get the advantages for themselves and thereby deny them to others. We should also look at how those who were the victims of such maldistribution manoeuvred, first of all to minimize their losses in the operation of the system, and secondly to transform this system which was responsible for such manifest injustices.

How in historical capitalism did people, groups of people, conduct their political struggles? Politics is about changing power relations in a direction more favourable to one's interests and thereby redirecting social processes. Its successful pursuit requires finding levers of change that permit the most advantage for the least input. The structure of historical capitalism has been such that the most effective levers of political adjustment were the state-structures, whose very construction was itself, as we have seen, one of the central institutional achievements of historical capitalism. It is thus no accident that the control of state power, the conquest of state power if necessary, has been the central strategic objective of all the major actors in the political arena throughout the history of modern capitalism.

The crucial importance of state power for economic processes, even if defined very narrowly is striking the moment one looks closely at how the system actually operated. The first and most elementary element of state power was territorial jurisdiction. States had boundaries. These boundaries were juridically determined, partly by statutory proclamation on the part of the state in question, partly by diplomatic recognition on the part of other states. To be sure, boundaries could be, and regularly were, contested; that is, the juridical recognitions coming from the two sources (the state itself and other states) were conflicting. Such differences were ultimately resolved either by adjudication or by force (and a resulting eventual acquiescence). Many disputes endured a latent form for very long periods, though very few such disputes survived more than a generation. What is crucial was the continuing ideological presumption on everyone's part that such disputes could and would be resolved eventually. What was conceptually impermissible in the modern state-system was an explicit recognition of permanent overlapping jurisdictions. Sovereignty as a concept was based on the Aristotelian law of the excluded middle.

This philosophical-juridical doctrine made it possible to fix responsibility for the control of movement across frontiers, in and out of given states. Each state had formal jurisdiction over its own frontiers of the movement of goods, money-capital, and labour-power. Hence each state could affect to some degree the modalities by which the social division of labour of the capitalist world-economy operated. Furthermore, each state could constantly adjust these mechanisms simply by changing the rules governing the flow of the factors of production across its own frontiers.

We normally discuss such frontier controls in terms of the antinomy between total absence of controls (free trade) and total absence of free movement (autarky). In fact, for most countries and for most moments of time, state policy has lain in practice between these two extremes. Furthermore, the policies have been quite specifically different for the movement

of goods, of money-capital, and of labour-power. In general, the movement of labour-power has been more restricted than the movement of goods and of money-capital.

From the point of view of a given producer located somewhere on a commodity chain, freedom of movement was desirable whilst this producer was economically competitive with other producers of the same goods in the world market. But when this was not the case, various boundary constraints against rival producers could raise the latter's costs and benefit an otherwise less efficient producer. Since, by definition, in a market in which there were multiple producers of any given good, a majority would be less efficient than a minority, there has existed a constant pressure for mercantilist constraints on free movement across frontiers. Since however the minority who were more efficient were relatively wealthy and powerful, there has been a constant counter-pressure to open frontiers, or more specifically, to open some frontiers. Hence the first great struggle—a ferocious and continuing one—has been over the frontier policy of states. Since furthermore any given set of producers (but particularly big and powerful ones) were directly affected by the state frontier policies of not only the states in which their economic base was physically located (which may or may not have been the ones of which they were citizens) but also those of many other states, given economic producers have been interested in pursuing political objectives simultaneously in several, indeed often in very many, states. The concept that one ought to restrict one's political involvement to one's own state was deeply antithetical to those who were pursuing the accumulation of capital for its own sake.

One way, of course, to affect the rules about what may or may not cross frontiers, and under what terms, was to change the actual frontiers—through total incorporation by one state of another (unification, *Anschluss*, colonization), through seizure of some territory, through secession or decolonization. The fact that frontier changes have had immediate impacts on the patterns of the social division of labour in the world-economy has been central to the considerations of all those who favoured or opposed particular frontier changes. The fact that ideological mobilizations around the definition of nations could make more, or less, possible certain specific frontier changes has given immediate economic content to nationalist movements, insofar as participants and others presumed the likelihood of specific state policies following upon the projected frontier changes.

The second element of state power of fundamental concern to the operations of historical capitalism was the legal right of states to determine the rules governing the social relations of production within their territorial jurisdiction. Modern state-structures arrogated to themselves this right to revoke or amend any customary set of relations. As a matter of law the states recognized no constraints on their legislative scope other than those that were self-imposed. Even where particular state constitutions paid ideological lip service to constraints deriving from religious or natural law doctrines, they reserved to some constitutionally-defined body or person the right to interpret these doctrines.

This right to legislate the modes of labour control was by no means merely theoretical. States have regularly used these rights, often in ways that involved radical transformations of existing patterns. As we would expect, in historical capitalism, states have legislated in ways that increased the commodification of labour power, by abolishing various kinds of customary constraint on the movement of workers from one kind of employment to another. They furthermore imposed on the work-force fiscal cash obligations which often forced certain workers to engage in wage-labour. But, on the other hand, as we have already seen, the states by their legal actions often also discouraged full-fledged proletarianization by imposing residential limitations or insisting that the kin group retain certain kinds of welfare obligations to its members.

The states controlled the relations of production. They first legalized, later outlawed, particular forms of coerced labour (slavery, public labour obligations, indenture, etc.). They created rules governing wage-labour contracts, including guarantees of the contract, and minimum and maximum reciprocal obligations. They decreed the limits of the geographical mobility of the labour force, not only across their frontiers but within them.

All these state decisions were taken with direct reference to the economic implications for the accumulation of capital. This can be easily verified by going through the enormous number of debates, recorded as they occurred, over alternative statutory or administrative choices. Furthermore, the states have regularly spent considerable energy in enforcing their regulations against recalcitrant groups, most particularly recalcitrant work-forces. Workers were seldom left free to ignore legal constraints on their actions. Quite the contrary—worker rebellion, individual or collective, passive or active, has usually brought forth a ready repressive response from the state-machineries. To be sure, organized working-class movements were able, in time, to set certain limitations to repressive activity, as well as ensure that the governing rules were modified somewhat in their favour, but such movements obtained these results largely by their ability to affect the political composition of the state-machineries.

A third element in the power of the states has been the power to tax. Taxation was by no means an invention of historical capitalism; previous political structures also used taxation as a source of revenue for the state-machineries. But historical capitalism transformed taxation in two ways. Taxation became the main (indeed overwhelming) regular source of state revenue, as opposed to state revenue deriving from irregular requisition by force from persons inside or outside the formal jurisdiction of the state (including requisition from other states). Secondly, taxation has been a steadily expanding phenomenon over the historical development of the capitalist world-economy as a percentage of total value created or accumulated. This has meant that the states have been important in terms of the resources they controlled, because the resources not only permitted them to further the accumulation of capital but were also themselves distributed and thereby entered directly or indirectly into the further accumulation of capital.

Taxation was a power which focused hostility and resistance upon the state-structure itself, as a sort of disincarnated villain, which was seen as appropriating the fruits of the labours of others. What must always be borne in mind is that there were forces outside the government pushing for particular taxations because the process would either result in direct redistribution to them, or permit the government to create external economies which would improve their economic position, or penalize others in ways that would be economically favourable to the first group. In short, the power to tax was one of the most immediate ways in which the state directly assisted the process of the accumulation of capital in favour of some groups rather than others.

The redistributive powers of the state have been discussed for the most part only in terms of their equalization potential.

This is the theme of the welfare state. But redistribution has in fact been far more widely used as a mechanism to polarize distribution than to make real incomes converge. There are three main mechanisms that have increased the polarization of rewards *over and above* that polarization already resulting from the ongoing operations of the capitalist market.

Governments first of all have been able to amass, through the taxation process, large sums of capital which they have redistributed to persons or groups, already large holders of capital, through official subsidies. These subsidies have taken the form of outright grants, usually on thin excuses of public service (involving essentially overpayments for services). But they have also taken the less direct form of the state bearing the costs of product development which could presumably be amortized by later profitable sales, only to turn over the economic activity to non-governmental entrepreneurs at nominal cost at precisely the point of completion of the costly developmental phase.

Secondly, governments have been able to amass large sums of capital through formally legal and often legitimated channels of taxation which have then becoming sitting ducks for large-scale illegitimate but de facto unconstrained abscondings of public funds. Such theft of public revenues as well as the correlate corrupt private taxation procedures have been a major source of private accumulation of capital throughout historical capitalism.

Finally, governments have redistributed to the wealthy by utilizing the principle of the individualization of profit but the socialization of risk. Over the whole history of the capitalist system, the larger the risk—and the losses—the more likely it has been for governments to step in to prevent bankruptcies and even to restitute losses if only because of the financial turmoil they wished to avoid.

While these practices of anti-egalitarian redistribution have been the shameful side of state power (shameful in the sense that governments were somewhat embarrassed about these activities and sought to keep them hidden), the provision of social overhead capital by governments has been openly flaunted, and indeed advocated as an essential role of the state in the maintenance of historical capitalism.

Expenditures crucial to the reduction of costs of multiple groups of owner-producers—that is, the basic energy, transport, and informational infrastructure of the world-economy—have largely been developed and supported by public funds. While it has no doubt been the case that most persons have derived *some* benefit from such social overhead capital, it has not been the case that all have derived equal benefit. The advantage has accrued disproportionately to those already large holders of capital while being paid out of a far more egalitarian system of taxation. Hence social overhead capital construction has served to further the accumulation of capital and its concentration.

Finally, states have monopolized, or sought to monopolize, armed force. While police forces were geared largely to the maintenance of internal order (that is, the acceptance by the work force of their allotted roles and rewards), armies have been mechanisms whereby producers in one state have been able to affect directly the possibilities that their competitors located in other states have had to invoke the protective covering of their own state-machineries. This is fact brings us to the last feature of state power which has been crucial. While the kinds of power each state has exercised have been similar, the degree of power given state-machineries have had has varied enormously. States have been located in a hierarchy of effective power which can be measured neither by the size and coherence of their bureaucracies and armies nor by their ideological formulations about themselves but by their effective capacities over time to further the concentration of accumulated capital within their frontiers as against those rival states. This effective capacity has involved the ability to constrain hostile military forces; the ability to enact advantageous regulations at home and to prevent other states from doing the same; and the ability to constrain their own work forces and to undermine the capacity of rivals to do as well. The true measurement of their strength is in the medium-term economic outcome. The overt use of force by the state-machinery to control the internal work force, a costly and destabilizing technique, is more often the sign of its weakness than its strength. Truly strong state-machineries have been able, by one means or another, to control their work-forces by subtler mechanisms.

Thus there are many different ways in which the state has been a crucial mechanism for the maximal accumulation of capital. According to its ideology, capitalism was supposed to involve the activity of private entrepreneurs freed from the interference of state-machineries. In practice, however, this has never been really true anywhere. It is idle to speculate whether capitalism could have flourished without the active role of the modern state. In historical capitalism, capitalists relied upon their ability to utilize state-machineries to their advantage in the various ways we have outlined.

A second ideological myth has been that of state sovereignty. The modern state was never a completely autonomous political entity. The states developed and were shaped as integral parts of an interstate system, which was a set of rules within which the states had to operate and a set of legitimizations without which states could not survive. From the point of view of the state-machineries of any given state, the interstate system represented constraints on its will. These were to be found in the practices of diplomacy, in the formal rules governing jurisdictions and contracts (international law), and in the limits on how and under what circumstances warfare might be conducted. All of these constraints ran counter to the official ideology of sovereignty. Sovereignty however was never really intended to mean total autonomy. The concept was rather meant to indicate that there existed limits on the legitimacy of interference by one state-machinery in the operations of another.

The rules of the interstate system were of course not enforced by consent or consensus, but by the willingness and the ability of the stronger states to impose these restrictions, first upon the weaker states, and second upon each other. The states, remember, were located in a hierarchy of power. The very existence of this hierarchy provided the major limitation on the autonomy of states. To be sure, the overall situation could tip towards the disappearance of the power of the states altogether to the extent that the hierarchy was constructed with a pyramidal peak rather than a plateau at the top. This possibility was not hypothetical as the dynamic of the concentration of military power led to recurrent thrusts to transform the interstate system into a world-empire.

If such thrusts never succeeded in historical capitalism, it was because the structural base of the economic system and the clearly-perceived interests of the major accumulators of capital were fundamentally opposed to a transformation of the world-economy into a world-empire.

First of all, the accumulation of capital was a game in which there was constant incentive for competitive entry, and thus there was always some dispersion of the most profitable productive activities. Hence at any time numerous states tended to have an economic base that made them relatively strong. Secondly, accumulators of capital in any given state utilized their own state structures to assist them in the accumulation of capital, but they also needed some lever of control *against* their own state-structures. For if their state-machinery became too strong, it might, for reasons of internal political equilibrium, feel free to respond to internal egalitarian pressures. Against this threat, accumulators of capital needed the threat of circumventing their own state-machinery by making alliances with other state-machineries. This threat was only possible as long as no one state dominated the whole.

These considerations formed the objective basis of the so-called balance of power, by which we mean that the numerous strong and medium-strong states in the interstate system at any given time have tended to maintain alliances (of if need be, shift them) so that no single state could successfully conquer all the others.

That the balance of power was maintained by more than political ideology can be seen if we look at the three instances in which one of the strong states achieved temporarily a period of relative dominance over the others—a relative dominance that we may call hegemony. The three instances are the hegemony of the United Provinces (Netherlands) in the mid-seventeenth century, that of Great Britain in the mid-nineteenth, and that of the United States in the mid-twentieth.

In each case, hegemony came after the defeat of a military pretender to conquest (the Hapsburgs, France, Germany). Each hegemony was sealed by a 'world war'—a massive, land-centred, highly destructive, thirty-year-long intermittent struggle involving all the major military powers of the time. These were respectively the Thirty Years' War of 1618-48, the Napoleonic Wars (1792-1815), and the twentieth-century conflicts between 1914 and 1945 which should properly be conceived as a single long 'world war'. It is to be noted that, in each case, the victor had been primarily a maritime power prior to 'world war', but had transformed itself into a land power in order to win this war against a historically strong land power which seemed to be trying to transform the world-economy into a world-empire.

The basis of the victory was not however military. The primary reality was economic: the ability of accumulators of capital located in the particular states to outcompete all others in all three major economic spheres—agro-industrial production, commerce, and finance. Specifically, for brief periods, the accumulators of capital in the hegemonic state were more efficient than their competitors located in other strong states, and thus won markets even within the latter's 'home' areas. Each of these hegemonies was brief. Each came to an end largely for economic reasons more than for politico-military reasons. In each case, the temporary triple economic advantage came up against two hard rocks of capitalist reality. First, the factors that made for greater economic efficiency could always be copied by others—not by the truly weak but those who had medium strength—and latecomers to any given economic process tend to have the advantage of not having to amortize older stock. Secondly, the hegemonic power had every interest in maintaining uninterrupted economic activity and therefore tended to buy labour peace with internal redistribution. Over time, this led to reduced competitiveness thereby ending hegemony. In addition, the conversion of the hegemonic power to one with far-flung land and maritime military 'responsibilities' involved a growing economic burden on the hegemonic state, thus undoing its pre-'world war' low level expenditure on the military.

Hence, the balance of power—constraining both the weak states and the strong—was not a political epiphenomenon which could be easily undone. It was rooted in the very ways in which capital was accumulated in historical capitalism. Nor was the balance of power merely a relationship between state-machineries, because the internal actors within any given state regularly acted beyond their own boundaries either directly or via alliances with actors elsewhere. Therefore, in assessing the politics of any given state, the internal/external distinction is quite formal and it is not too helpful to our understanding of how the political struggles actually occurred.

But who in fact was struggling with whom? This is not as obvious a question as one might think, because of the contradictory pressures within historical capitalism. The most elementary struggle, and in some ways the most obvious, was that between the small group of great beneficiaries of the system and the large group of its victims. This struggle goes by many names and under many guises. Whenever the lines have been drawn fairly clearly between the accumulators of capital and their work force within any given state, we have tended to call this a class struggle between capital and labour. Such class struggles took place in two locales—the economic arena (both at the locus of actual work and in the larger amorphous 'market') and the political arena. It is clear that in the economic arena there has been a direct, logical, and immediate conflict of interests. The larger the remuneration of the workforce the less surplus was left as 'profit'. To be sure, this conflict has been often softened by longer-term, larger-scale considerations. Both the particular accumulator of capital and his work-force shared interests against other pairings elsewhere in the system. And greater remuneration to work-forces could under certain circumstances return to the accumulators of capital as deferred profit, via the increased global cash purchasing power in the world-economy. Nonetheless, none of these other considerations could ever eliminate the fact that the division of a given surplus was a zero-sum, and thus the tension has been perforce a continuing one. It has therefore found continuing expression in competition for political power within the various states.

Since, however, as we know, the process of the accumulation of capital has led to its concentration in some geographic zones, since the unequal exchange which accounts for this has been made possible by the existence of an interstate system containing a hierarchy of states, and since state-machineries have some limited power to alter the operations of the system, the struggle between worldwide accumulators of capital and the worldwide work-force has found considerable expression too in the efforts of various groups to come to power within given (weaker) states in order to utilize state power against accumulators of capital located in stronger states. Whenever this has occurred, we have tended to speak of anti-imperialist struggles. No doubt, here too, the question was often obscured by the fact that the lines internal to each of the two states involved did not always coincide perfectly with the underlying thrust of the class struggle in the world-economy as a whole. Some accumulators of capital in the weaker state and some elements of the work-force in the stronger found short-term advantages in defining the political issues in purely national rather than in class-national terms. But great mobilizational thrusts of 'anti-imperialist' movements were never possible, and therefore even limited objectives were seldom achieved, if the class content of the struggle were not there and used, at least implicitly, as an ideological theme.

We have noted also that the process of ethnic-group formation was integrally linked with that of labour-force formation in given states, serving as a rough code of position in the economic structures. Therefore, wherever this has occurred more sharply or circumstances have forced more acute short-term pressures on survival, the conflict between the accumulators of capital and the more oppressed segments of the work-force have tended to take the form of linguistic-racial-cultural struggles, since such descriptors have a high correlation with class membership. Wherever and whenever this has occurred, we have tended to talk of ethnic or nationality struggles. Exactly, however, as in the case of the anti-imperialist struggles, these struggles were rarely successful unless they were able to mobilize the sentiments that emerged out of the underlying class struggle for the appropriation of the surplus produced within the capitalist system.

Nonetheless, if we pay attention only to the class struggle, because it is both obvious and fundamental, we shall lose from view another political struggle that has absorbed at least as much time and energy in historical capitalism. For the capitalist system is a system that has pitted all accumulators of capital against one another. Since the mode by which one pursued the endless accumulation of capital was that of realizing the profits coming from economic activity against the competitive efforts of others, no individual entrepreneur could ever be more than the fickle ally of any other entrepreneur, on pain of being eliminated from the competitive scene altogether.

Entrepreneur against entrepreneur, economic sector against economic sector, the entrepreneurs located in one state, or ethnic group, against those in another—the struggle has been by definition ceaseless. And this ceaseless struggle has constantly taken a political form, precisely because of the central role of the states in the accumulation of capital. Sometimes these struggles within states have merely been over personnel in the state-machineries and short-run state policies. Sometimes, however, they have been over larger 'constitutional' issues which determine the rules governing the conduct of shorter-run struggles, and thus the likelihood of one faction or another prevailing. Whenever these struggles were 'constitutional' in nature, they required greater ideological mobilization. In these cases, we heard talk of 'revolutions' and 'great reforms' and the losing sides were often given opprobrious (but analytically inappropriate) labels. To the extent that the political struggles for, say, 'democracy' or 'liberty' against 'feudalism' or 'tradition' have not been struggles of the working classes against capitalism, they have been essentially struggles among the accumulators of capital for the accumulation of capital. Such struggles were not the triumph of a 'progressive' bourgeoisie against reactionary strata but *intra*-bourgeois struggles.

Of course, using 'universalizing' ideological slogans about progress has been politically useful. It has been a way of associating class struggle mobilization to one side of intra-accumulator struggles. But such ideological advantage has often been a double-edged sword, unleashing passions and weakening repressive restraints in the class struggle. This was of course one of the ongoing dilemmas of the accumulators of capital in historical capitalism. They were forced by the operations of the system to act in class solidarity with one another against the efforts of the work-force to pursue its contrary interests, but simultaneously to fight each other ceaselessly in both the economic and political arenas. This is exactly what we mean by a contradiction within the system.

Many analysts, noticing that there are struggles other than class struggles which absorb much of the total political energy expended, have concluded that class analysis is of dubious relevance to the understanding of political struggle. This is a curious inference. It would seem more sensible to conclude that these non-class-based political struggles, that is, struggles among accumulators for political advantage, are evidence of a severe structural political weakness in the accumulator class in its ongoing worldwide class struggle.

These political struggles can be rephrased as struggles to shape the institutional structures of the capitalist world-economy so as to construct the kind of world market whose operation would automatically favour particular economic actors. The capitalist 'market' was never a given, and even less a constant. It was a creation that was regularly recreated and adjusted.

At any given time, the 'market' represented a set of rules or constraints resulting from the complex interplay of four major sets of institutions: the multiple states linked in an interstate system; the multiple 'nations', whether fully recognized or struggling for such public definition (and including those subnations, the 'ethnic groups'), in uneasy and uncertain relation to the states; the classes, in evolving occupational contour and in oscillating degrees of consciousness; and the income-pooling units engaged in common householding, combining multiple persons engaged in multiple forms of labour and obtaining income from multiple sources, in uneasy relationship to the classes.

There were no fixed lodestars in this constellation of institutional forces. There were no 'primordial' entities that tended to prevail against the institutional forms pressed for by the accumulators of capital in tandem with, and in opposition to, the struggle of the work-force to resist appropriation of their economic product. The boundaries of each variant of an institutional form, the 'rights' which it was legally and de facto able to sustain, varied from zone to zone of the world-economy, over both cyclical and secular time. If the careful analyst's head reels in regarding this institutional vortex, he can steer a clear path by remembering that in historical capitalism accumulators had no higher object than further accumulation, and that work-forces could therefore have no higher object than survival and reducing their burden. Once that is remembered, one is able to make a great deal of sense out of the political history of the modern world.

In particular, one can begin to appreciate in their complexity the circumlocutory and often paradoxical or contradictory positions of the anti-systemic movements that emerged in historical capitalism. Let us begin with the most elementary dilemma of all. Historical capitalism has operated within a world-economy but not within a world-state. Quite the contrary. As we have seen, structural pressures militated against any construction of a world-state. Within this system, we have underlined the crucial role of the multiple states—at once the most powerful political structures, and yet of limited power. Hence restructuring given states represented for work-forces at one and the same time the most promising path of improving their position, and a path of limited value.

We must begin by looking at what we might mean by an anti-systemic movement. The word movement implies some collective thrust of a more than momentary nature. In fact, of course, somewhat spontaneous protests or uprisings of work-forces have occurred in all known historical systems. They have served as safety-values for pent-up anger; or sometimes, somewhat more effectively, as mechanisms that have set minor limits to exploitative process. But generally speaking, rebellion as a technique has worked only at the margins of central authority, particularly when central bureaucracies were in phases of disintegration.

The structure of historical capitalism changed some of these givens. The fact that states were located in an interstate system meant that the repercussions of rebellions or uprisings were felt, often quite rapidly, beyond the confines of the immediate political jurisdiction within which they occurred. So-called 'outside' forces therefore had strong motives to come to the aid of assailed state-machineries. This made rebellions more difficult. On the other hand, the intrusion of the accumulators of capital, and hence of state-machineries, into the daily life of the work-forces was far more intensive in general under historical capitalism than under previous historical systems. The endless accumulation of capital led to repeated pressures to restructure the organization (and location) of work, to increase the amount of absolute labour, and to bring about the psycho-social reconstruction of the work-forces. In this sense, for most of the world's work-forces, the disruption, the discombobulation, and the exploitation was even greater. At the same time, the social disruption undermined placatory modes of socialization. All in all, therefore, the motivations to rebel were strengthened, despite the fact that the possibilities of success were perhaps objectively lessened.

It was this extra strain which led to the great innovation in the technology of rebellion that was developed in historical capitalism. This innovation was the concept of permanent organization. It is only in the nineteenth century that we begin to see the creation of continuing, bureaucratized structures in their two great historical variants: labour-socialist movements, and nationalist movements. Both kinds of movement talked a universal language—essentially that of the French Revolution: liberty, equality, and fraternity. Both kinds of movement clothed themselves in the ideology of the Enlightment—the inevitability of progress, that is human emancipation justified by inherent human rights. Both kinds of movement appealed to the future against the past, the new against the old. Even when tradition was invoked, it was as the basis of a renaissance, a rebirth.

Each of the two kinds of movement had, it is true, a different focus, and hence at first a different locus. The labour-socialist movements focused on the conflicts between the urban, landless, wage workers (the proletariat) and the owners of the economic structures in which they worked (the bourgeoisie). These movements insisted that the allocation of reward for work was fundamentally inegalitarian, oppressive, and unjust. It was natural that such movements should first emerge in those parts of the world-economy that had a significant industrial work-force—in particular, in western Europe.

The nationalist movements focused on the conflicts between the numerous 'oppressed peoples' (defined in terms of linguistic and/or religious characteristics) and the particular dominant 'peoples' of a given political jurisdiction, the former having far fewer political rights, economic opportunities, and legitimate forms of cultural expression than the latter. These movements insisted that the allocation of 'rights' was fundamentally inegalitarian, oppressive, and unjust. It was natural that such movements should first emerge in those semiperipheral regions of the world-economy, like the Austro-

Hungarian Empire, where the uneven assignment of ethno-national groups in the hierarchy of labour-force allocation was most obvious.

In general, up until quite recently, these two kinds of movement considered themselves very different from, sometimes even antagonistic to, the other. Alliances between them were seen as tactical and temporary. Yet from the beginning, it is striking the degree to which both kinds of movement shared certain structural similarities. In the first place, after considerable debate, both labour-socialist and nationalist movements made the basic decision to become organizations and the concurrent decision that their most important political objective was the seizure of state power (even when, in the case of some nationalist movements, this involved the creation of new state boundaries). Secondly, the decision on the strategy—the seizure of state power—required that these movements mobilize popular forces on the basis of an anti-systemic, that is, revolutionary, ideology. They were against the existing system—historical capitalism—which was built on the basic capital-labour, core-periphery structured inequalities that the movements were seeking to overcome.

Of course, in an unequal system, there are always two ways in which a low-ranking group can seek to get out of its low rank. It can seek to restructure the system such that all have equal rank. Or it can seek simply to move itself into a higher rank in the unequal distribution. As we know, anti-systemic movements, no matter how much they focused on egalitarian objectives, always included elements whose objective, initially or eventually, was merely to be 'upwardly mobile' within the existing hierarchy. The movements themselves have always been aware of this too. They have however tended to discuss this problem in terms of individual motivations: the pure of heart versus the betrayers of the cause. But when on analysis the 'betrayers of the cause' seem omnipresent in every particular instance of the movements as they have historically developed, one is led to look for structural rather than motivational explanations.

The key to the problem may in fact lie in the basic strategic decision to make the seizure of state power the pivot of the movement's activities. The strategy had two fundamental consequences. In the phase of mobilization, it pushed each movement towards entering into tactical alliances with groups that were in no way 'anti-systemic' in order to reach its strategic objective. These alliances modified the structure of the anti-systemic movements themselves, even in the mobilization stage. Even more importantly, the strategy eventually succeeded in many cases. Many of the movements achieved partial or even total state power. These successful movements were then confronted with the realities of the limitations of state power within the capitalist world-economy. They found that they were constrained by the functioning of the interstate system to exercise their power in ways that muted the 'anti-systemic' objectives that were their raison d'être.

This seems so obvious that one must then wonder why the movements based their strategy on such a seemingly self-defeating objective. The answer was quite simple: given the political structure of historical capitalism, they had little choice. There seemed to be no more promising alternative strategy. The seizure of state power at least promised to change the balance of power between contending groups somewhat. That is to say, the seizure of power represented a *reform* of the system. The reforms in fact did improve the situation, but always at the price of also strengthening the system.

Can we therefore summarize the work of the world's anti-systemic movements for over one hundred and fifty years as simply the strengthening of historical capitalism via reformism? No, but that is because the politics of historical capitalism was more than the politics of the various states. It has been the politics of the interstate system as well. The anti-systemic movements existed from the beginning not only individually but also as a collective whole, albeit never bureaucratically organized. (The multiple internationals have never included the totality of these movements.) A key factor in the strength of any given movement has always been the existence of other movements.

Other movements have provided any given movement with three kinds of support. The most obvious is material; helpful, but perhaps of least significance. A second is diversionary support. The ability of a given strong state to intervene against an anti-systemic movement located in a weaker state, for example, was always a function of how many other things were on its immediate political agenda. The more a given state was preoccupied with a local anti-systemic movement, the less ability it had to be occupied with a faraway anti-systemic movement. The third and most fundamental support is at the level of collective mentalities. Movements learned from each other's errors and were encouraged by each other's tactical successes. And the efforts of the movements worldwide affected the basic worldwide political ambiance—the expectations, the analysis of possibilities.

As the movements grew in number, in history, and in tactical successes, they seemed stronger as a collective phenomenon, and because they seemed stronger they were. The greater collective strength worldwide served as a check on 'revisionist' tendencies of movements in state power—no more, but no less, than that—and this has been greater in its effect on undermining the political stability of historical capitalism than the sum of the system-strengthening effects of the seizure of state power by successive individual movements.

Finally, one other factor has come into play. As the two varieties of anti-systemic movements have spread (the labour-socialist movements from a few strong states to all others, the nationalist movements from a few peripheral zones to everywhere else), the distinction between the two kinds of movement has become increasingly blurred. Labour-socialist movements have found that nationalist themes were central to their mobilization efforts and their exercise of state power. But nationalist movements have discovered the inverse. In order to mobilize effectively and govern, they had to canalize the concerns of the work-force for egalitarian restructuring. As the themes began to overlap heavily and the distinctive organizational formats tended to disappear or coalesce into a single structure, the strength of anti-systemic movements, especially as a worldwide collective whole, was dramatically increased.

One of the strengths of the anti-systemic movements is that they have come to power in a large number of states. This has changed the ongoing politics of the world-system. But this strength has also been a weakness, since the so-called post-revolutionary regimes continue to function as part of the social division of labour of historical capitalism. They have thereby operated, willy nilly, under the relentless pressures of the drive for the endless accumulation of capital. The political consequence internally has been the continued exploitation of the labour-force, if in a reduced and ameliorated form in many instances. This has led to internal tensions paralleling those found in states that were not 'post-revolutionary', and this in turn has bred the emergence of new anti-systemic movements within these states. The struggle for the benefits has been going on both within these post-revolutionary states and everywhere else, because, within the framework of the capitalist world-economy, the imperatives of accumulation have operated *throughout* the sytem. Changes in state structures have altered the politics of accumulation; they have not yet been able to end them.

Initially, we postponed the questions: how real have been the benefits in historical capitalism? how great has been the change in the quality of life? It should be clear now that there is no simple answer. 'For whom?', we must ask. Historical capitalism has involved a monumental creation of material goods, but also a monumental polarization of reward. Many have benefited enormously, but many more have known a substantial reduction in their real total incomes and in the quality of their lives. The polarization has of course also been spatial, and hence it has seemed in some areas not to exist. That too has been the consequence of a struggle for the benefits. The geography of benefit has frequently shifted, thus masking the reality of polarization. But over the whole of the time-space zone encompassed by historical capitalism, the endless accumulation of capital has meant the incessant widening of the real gap.

3.
Truth as Opiate:
Rationality
and Rationalization

Historical capitalism has been, we know, Promethean in its aspirations. Although scientific and technological change has been a constant of human historical activity, it is only with historical capitalism that Prometheus, always there, has been 'unbound', in David Landes's phrase. The basic collective image we now have of this scientific culture of historical capitalism is that it was propounded by noble knights against the staunch resistance of the forces of 'traditional', non-scientific culture. In the seventeenth century, it was Galileo against the Church; in the twentieth, the 'modernizer' against the mullah. At all points, it was said to have been 'rationality' versus 'superstition', and 'freedom' versus 'intellectual oppression'. This was presumed to be parallel to (even identical with) the revolt in the arena of the political economy of the bourgeois entrepreneur against the aristocratic landlord.

This basic image of a worldwide cultural struggle has had a hidden premiss, namely one about temporality. 'Modernity' was assumed to be temporally new, whereas 'tradition' was temporally old and prior to modernity; indeed, in some strong versions of the imagery, tradition was ahistorical and therefore virtually eternal. This premiss was historically false and therefore fundamentally misleading. The multiple cultures, the multiple 'traditions' that have flourished within the time-space boundaries of historical capitalism, have been no more primordial than the multiple institutional frameworks. They are largely the creation of the modern world, part of its ideological scaffolding. Links of the various 'traditions' to groups and ideologies that predate historical capitalism have existed, of course, in the sense that they have often been constructed using some historical and intellectual materials already existent. Furthermore, the assertion of such transhistorical links has played an important role in the cohesiveness of groups in their politico-economic struggles within historical capitalism. But, if we wish to understand the cultural forms these struggles take, we cannot afford to take 'traditions' at their face value, and in particular we cannot afford to assume that 'traditions' are in fact traditional.

It was in the interests of those who wished to facilitate the accumulation of capital, that work-forces be created in the right places and at the lowest possible levels of remuneration. We have already discussed how the lower rates of pay for peripheral economic activities in the world-economy were made possible by the creation of households in which wage labour played a minority role as a source of income. One way in which such households were 'created', that is, pressured to structure themselves, was the 'ethnicization' of community life in historical capitalism. What we mean by 'ethnic groups' are sizeable groups of people to whom were reserved certain occupational/economic roles in relation to other such groups living in geographic proximity. The outward symbolization of such labour-force allocation was the distinctive 'culture' of the ethnic group—its religion, its language, its 'values', its particular set of everyday behaviour patterns.

Of course, I am not suggesting that there was anything like a perfect caste system in historical capitalism. But, provided we keep our occupational categories sufficiently broad, I am suggesting that there is, and always has been, a rather high correlation between ethnicity and occupation/economic role throughout the various time-space zones of historical capitalism. I am further suggesting that these labour-force allocations have varied over time, and that as they varied, so did ethnicity—in terms of the boundaries and defining cultural features of the group, and further that there is almost no correlation between present-day ethnic labour-force allocation and the patterns of the purported ancestors of present-day ethnic groups in periods prior to historical capitalism.

The ethnicization of the world work-force has had three main consequences that have been important for the functioning of the world-economy. First of all, it has made possible the reproduction of the work-force, not in the sense of providing sufficient income for the survival of groups but in the sense of providing sufficient workers in each category at appropriate levels of income expectations in terms both of total amounts and of the forms the household income would take. Furthermore, precisely because the work-force was ethnicized, its allocation was flexible. Large-scale geographical and occupational mobility has been made easier, not more difficult, by ethnicity. Under the pressure of changing economic conditions, all that was required to change work-force allocation was for some enterprising individuals to take the lead in geographical or occupational resettlement, and to be rewarded for it; this promptly exerted a natural 'pull' on other members of the ethnic group to transfer their locations in the world-economy.

Secondly, ethnicization has provided an in-built training mechanism of the work-force, ensuring that a large part of the socialization in occupational tasks would be done within the framework of ethnically-defined households and not at the cost of either employers of wage-workers, or the states.

Thirdly, and probably most important, ethnicization has encrusted ranking of occupational/economic roles, providing an easy code for overall income distribution—clothed with the legitimization of 'tradition'.

It is this third consequence that has been elaborated in greatest detail and has formed one of the most significant pillars of historical capitalism, institutional racism. What we mean by racism has little to do with the xenophobia that existed in various prior historical systems. Xenophobia was literally fear of the 'stranger'. Racism within historical capitalism had nothing to do with 'strangers'. Quite the contrary. Racism was the mode by which various segments of the work-force within the same economic structure were constrained to relate to each other. Racism was the ideological justification for the hierarchization of the work-force and its highly unequal distributions of reward. What we mean by racism is that set of ideological statements combined with that set of continuing practices which have had the consequence of maintaining a high correlation of ethnicity and work-force allocation over time. The ideological statements have been in the form of allegations that genetic and/or long-lasting 'cultural' traits of various groups are the major cause of differential allocation to positions in the economic structures. However, the beliefs that certain groups were 'superior' to others in certain characteristics relevant to performance in the economic arena always came into being after, rather than before, the location of these groups in the work-force. Racism has always been post hoc. It has been asserted that those who have been economically and politically oppressed are culturally 'inferior'. If, for any reason, the locus in the economic hierarchy changed, the locus in the social hierarchy tended to follow (with some lag, to be sure, since it always took a generation or two to eradicate the effect of previous socialization).

Racism has served as an overall ideology justifying inequality. But it has been much more. It has served to socialize groups into their own role in the economy. The attitudes inculcated (the prejudices, the overtly discriminatory behaviour in everyday life) served to establish the framework of appropriate and legitimate behaviour for oneself and for others in one's own household and ethnic group. Racism, just like sexism, functioned as a self-suppressive ideology, fashioning expectations and limiting them.

Racism was certainly not only self-suppressive; it was oppressive. It served to keep low-ranking groups in line, and utilize middle-ranking groups as the unpaid soldiers of the world police system. In this way, not only were the financial costs of the political structures reduced significantly, but the ability of anti-systemic groups to mobilize wide populations was rendered more difficult, since racism structually set victims against victims.

Racism was not a simple phenomenon. There was in a sense a basic world-wide fault line, marking off relative status in the world-system as a whole. This was the 'colour' line. What was 'white' or upper stratum has of course been a social and not a physiological phenomenon, as should be evident by the historically-shifting position, in worldwide (and national) socially-defined 'colour lines', of such groups as southern Europeans, Arabs, Latin American mestizos, and East Asians.

Colour (or physiology) was an easy tag to utilize, since it is inherently hard to disguise, and, insofar as it has been historically convenient, given the origins of historical capitalism in

Europe, it has been utilized. But whenever it was not convenient, it has been discarded or modified in favour of other identifying characteristics. In many particular places, the sets of identifiers have thus become quite complex. When one considers the additional fact that the social division of labour was constantly evolving, ethnic/racial identification turned out to be a highly unstable basis for delineating the boundaries of the existing social groups. Groups came and went and changed their self-definitions with considerable ease (and were perceived by others as having different boundaries with equal ease). But the volatility of any given group's boundaries was not inconsistent with, indeed was probably a function of, the persistence of an overall hierarchy of groups, that is, the ethnicization of the world work-force.

Racism has thus been a cultural pillar of historical capitalism. Its intellectual vacuity has not prevented it from unleashing terrible cruelties. Nonetheless, given the rise of the world's anti-systemic movements in the past fifty to one hundred years, it has recently been under sharp attack. Indeed, today racism in its crude variants is undergoing some delegitimization at the world level. Racism, however, has not been the only ideological pillar of historical capitalism. Racism has been of greatest importance in construction and reproduction of appropriate work forces. Their reproduction nonetheless was insufficient to permit the endless accumulation of capital. Work-forces could not be expected to perform efficiently and continuously unless they were managed by cadres. Cadres too have had to be created, socialized, reproduced. The primary ideology that operated to create, socialize, and reproduce them was not the ideology of racism. It was that of universalism.

Universalism is an epistemology. It is a set of beliefs about what is knowable and how it can be known. The essence of this view is that there exist meaningful general statements about the world—the physical world, the social world—that are universally and permanently true, and that the object of science is the search for these general statements in a form that eliminates all so-called subjective, that is, all historically-constrained, elements from its formulation.

The belief in universalism has been the keystone of the ideological arch of historical capitalism. Universalism is a faith, as well as an epistemology. It requires not merely respect but reverence for the elusive but allegedly real phenomenon of truth. The universities have been both the workshops of the ideology and the temples of the faith. Harvard emblazons *Veritas* on its escutcheon. While it has always been asserted that one could never know truth definitively—this is what is supposed to distinguish modern science from medieval Western theology—it was also constantly asserted that the search for truth was the raison d'être of the university, and more widely of all intellectual activity. Keats, to justify art, told us that 'truth is beauty, beauty truth.' In the United States, a favourite political justification of civil liberties is that truth can only be known as a result of the interplay that occurs in the 'free market-place of ideas'.

Truth as a cultural ideal has functioned as an opiate, perhaps the only serious opiate of the modern world. Karl Marx said that religion was the opiate of the masses. Raymond Aron retorted that Marxist ideas were in turn the opiate of the intellectuals. There is perspicacity in both these polemical thrusts. But is perspicacity truth? I wish to suggest that perhaps truth has been the real opiate, of both the masses and the intellectuals. Opiates, to be sure, are not unremittingly evil. They ease pain. They enable people to escape from hard realities when they fear that confrontation with reality can only precipitate inevitable loss or decline. But nonetheless most of us do not recommend opiates. Neither Marx nor Raymond Aron did. In most states and for most purposes they are illegal.

Our collective education has taught us that the search for truth is a disinterested virtue when in fact it is a self-interested rationalization. The search for truth, proclaimed as the cornerstone of progress, and therefore of well-being, has been at the very least consonant with the maintenance of a hierarchical, unequal social structure in a number of specific respects. The processes involved in the expansion of the capitalist world-economy—the peripheralization of economic structures, the creation of weak state structures participating in and constrained by an interstate system—involved a number of pressures at the level of culture: Christian proselytization; the imposition of European language; instruction in specific technologies and mores; changes in the legal codes. Many of these changes were made manu militari. Others were achieved by the persuasion of 'educators', whose authority was ultimately backed by military force. That is that complex of processes we sometimes label 'westernization', or even more arrogantly 'modernization', and which was legitimated by the desirability of sharing both the fruits of and faith in the ideology of universalism.

There were two main motives behind these enforced cultural changes. One was economic efficiency. If given persons were expected to perform in given ways in the economic arenas, it was efficient both to teach them the requisite cultural norms and to eradicate competing cultural norms. The second was political security. It was believed that if the so-called elites of peripheral areas were 'westernized', they would be separated from their 'masses', and hence less likely to revolt—certainly less able to organize a following for revolts. This turned out to be a monumental miscalculation, but it was plausible and did work for a while. (A third motive was *hybris* on the part of the conquerors. I do not discount it, but it is not necessary to invoke it in order to account for the cultural pressures, which would have been just as great in its absence.)

Whereas racism served as a mechanism of world-wide control of direct producers, universalism served to direct the activities of the bourgeoisie of other states and various middle strata world-wide into channels that would maximize the close integration of production processes and the smooth operation of the interstate system, thereby facilitating the accumulation of capital. This required the creation of a world bourgeois cultural framework that could be grafted onto 'national' variations. This was particularly important in terms of science and technology, but also in the realm of political ideas and the social sciences.

The concept of a neutral 'universal' culture to which the cadres of the world division of labour would be 'assimilated' (the passive voice being important here) hence came to serve as one of the pillars of the world-system as it historically evolved. The exaltation of progress, and later of 'modernization', summarized this set of ideas, which served less as true norms of social action than as status-symbols of obeisance and of participation in the world's upper strata. The break from the supposedly culturally-narrow religious bases of knowledge in favour of supposedly trans-cultural scientific bases of knowledge served as the self-justification of a particularly pernicious form of cultural imperalism. It dominated in the name of intellectual liberation; it imposed in the name of scepticism.

The process of rationalization central to capitalism has required the creation of an intermediate stratum comprising the specialists of this rationalization, as administrators, technicians, scientists, educators. The very complexity of not only the technology but the social system has made it essential that this stratum be large and, over time, expanding. The funds that have been used to support it have been drawn from the global surplus, as extracted through entrepreneurs and states. In this elementary but fundamental sense these cadres have therefore been part of the bourgeoisie whose claim to participation in the sharing-out of the surplus has been given precise ideological form in the twentieth-century concept of human capital. Having relatively little real capital to transmit as the heritage of their household, such cadres have sought to guarantee succession by securing preferential access for their children to the educational channels which guarantee position. This preferential access has been conveniently presented as achievement, supposedly legitimated by a narrowly-defined 'equality of opportunity'.

Scientific culture thus became the fraternal code of the world's accumulators of capital. It served first of all to justify both their own activities and the differential rewards from which they benefited. It promoted technological innovation. It legitimated the harsh elimination of barriers to the expansion of productive efficiencies. It generated a form of progress that would be of benefit to all—if not immediately then eventually.

Scientific culture was more however than a mere rationalization. It was a form of socialization of the diverse elements that were the cadres of all the institutional structures that were needed. As a language common to cadres but not directly to the labour-force, it became also a means of class cohesion for the upper stratum, limiting the prospects or extent of rebellious activity on the part of cadres who might be so tempted. Furthermore, it was a flexible mechanism for the reproduction of these cadres. It lent itself to the concept known today as 'meritocracy', previously 'la carrière ouverte aux talents'. Scientific culture created a framework within which individual mobility was possible without threatening hierarchical work-force allocation. On the contrary, meritocracy reinforced hierarchy. Finally, meritocracy as an operation and scientific culture as an ideology created veils that hindered perception of the underlying operations of historical capitalism. The great emphasis on the rationality of scientific activity was the mask of the irrationality of endless accumulation.

Universalism and racism may seem on the surface strange bedfellows, if not virtually antithetical doctrines—one open, the other closed; one equalizing, the other polarizing; one inviting rational discourse, the other incarnating prejudice. Yet, since these two doctrines have spread and prevailed concomitantly with the evolution of historical capitalism, we should look more closely at the ways in which they may have been compatible.

There was a catch to universalism. It did not make its way as a free-floating ideology but as one propagated by those who held economic and political power in the world-system of historical capitalism. Universalism was offered to the world as a gift of the powerful to the weak. *Timeo Danaos et dona ferentes*! The gift itself harboured racism, for it gave the recipient two choices: accept the gift, thereby acknowledging that one was low on the hierarchy of achieved wisdom; refuse the gift, thereby denying oneself weapons that could reverse the unequal real power situation.

It is not strange that even the cadres who were being co-opted into privilege were deeply ambivalent about the message of universalism, vacillating between enthusiastic discipleship and a cultural rejection brought on by repugnance for racist assumptions. This ambivalence was expressed in the multiple movements of cultural 'renaissance'. The very word renaissance, which was widely used in many zones of the world, itself incarnated the ambivalence. By speaking of rebirth, one affirmed an era of prior cultural glory but one also acknowledged a cultural inferiority as of that moment. The word rebirth was itself copied from the specific cultural history of Europe.

One might have thought that the world's work-forces were more immune from this ambivalence, never having been invited to sup at the lord's table. In fact, however, the political expressions of the world's work-forces, the anti-systemic movements, have themselves been deeply imbued with the same ambivalence. The anti-systemic movements, as we have already remarked, clothed themselves in the ideology of the Enlightenment, itself a prime product of universalist ideology. They thereby lay for themselves the cultural trap in which they have remained ever since: seeking to undermine historical capitalism, using strategies and setting medium-term objectives that derived from the very 'ideas of the ruling classes' they sought to destroy.

The socialist variant of anti-systemic movements was, from the outset, committed to scientific progress. Marx, wishing to distinguish himself from others he denounced as 'utopians', asserted that he was advocating 'scientific socalism'. His writings laid emphasis on the ways in which capitalism was 'progressive'. The concept that socialism would come first in the most 'advanced' countries suggested a process whereby socialism would grow out of (as well as in reaction to) the further advancement of capitalism. The socialist revolution would thus emulate *and come after* the 'bourgeois revolution'. Some later theorists even argued that it was therefore the duty of socialists to assist in the bourgeois revolution in those countries in which it had not yet occurred.

The later differences between the Second and Third Internationals did not involve a disagreement over this epistemology, which both shared. Indeed, both Social-Democrats and Communists in power have tended to give great prority to the further development of the means of production. Lenin's slogan that 'Communism equals socialism plus electricity' still hangs today in enormous banners on the streets of Moscow. Insofar as these movements, once in power—Social-Democrats and Communists alike—implemented Stalin's slogans of 'socialism in one country', they thereby necessarily furthered the process of the commodification of everything that has been so essential to the global accumulation of capital. Insofar as they remained within the interstate system—indeed struggled to remain within it against all attempts to oust them—they accepted and furthered the world-wide reality of the dominance of the law of value. 'Socialist man' looked suspiciously like Taylorism run wild.

There have been of course 'socialist' ideologies which have purported to reject the universalism of the Enlightenment, and have advocated various 'indigenous' varieties of socalism for peripheral zones of the world-economy. To the extent that these formulations were more than mere rhetoric, they seemed to be de facto attempts to use as a base unit of the process of commodification not the new households that share income but larger communal entities that were, it was argued, more 'traditional'. By and large, these attempts, when serious, turned out to be fruitless. In any case, the mainstream of world socialist movements tended to denounce these attempts as non-socialist, as forms of a retrograde cultural nationalism.

At first view, the nationalist variety of anti-systemic movements, by the very centrality of their separatist themes, seemed less beholden to the ideology of universalism. A closer look, however, belies this impression. Certainly, nationalism inevitably had a cultural component, in which particular movements argued for the reinforcement of national 'traditions', a national language, often a religious heritage. But was cultural nationalism cultural resistance to the pressures of the accumulators of capital? In fact, two major elements of cultural nationalism moved in opposite directions. First, the unit chosen as the vehicle to contain the culture tended to be the state that was a member of the interstate system. It was most often this state that was invested with a 'national' culture. In virtually every case, this involved a distortion of cultural continuities, frequently very severe. In almost all cases, the assertion of a state-encased national culture inevitably involved as much suppression of continuities as reassertion of them. In all cases, it reinforced the state structures, and thus the interstate system, and historical capitalism as a world-system.

Secondly, a comparative look at the cultural reassertions among all these states makes clear that while they varied in form, they tended to be identical in content. The morphemes of the languages differed but the vocabulary list began to converge. The rituals and theologies of the world's religions might all have been reinvigorated but they began to be less different in actual content than previously. And the antecedents of scientificity were rediscovered under many different names. In short, much of cultural nationalism has been a gigantic charade. More than that, cultural nationalism like 'socialist culture' has often been a major stalwart of the universalist ideology of the modern world, purveying it to the world's work-forces in ways they found more palatable. In this sense, the anti-systemic movements have often served as the cultural intermediaries of the powerful to the weak, vitiating rather than crystallizing their deep-rooted sources of resistance.

The contradictions inherent in the state-seizure strategy of anti-systemic movements combined with their tacit acceptance of the universalist epistemology has had serious consequences for these movements. They have had to deal increasingly with the phenomenon of disillusionment, to which their major ideological response has been the reaffirmation of the central justification of historical capitalism: the automatic and inevitable quality of progress, or as it is now popular to say in the USSR the 'scientific-technological revolution'.

Beginning in the twentieth century, and with increasing vehemence since the 1960's, the theme of the 'civilizational project', as Anouar Abdel-Malek likes to call it, has begun to gain strength. While for many the new language of 'endogenous alternatives' has served as merely a verbal variant of old universalizing cultural nationalist themes, for others there is genuinely new epistemological content in the theme. The 'civilizational project' has reopened the question of whether transhistorical truths really exist. A form of truth, which reflected the power realities and economic imperatives of historical capitalism, has flourished and permeated the globe. That is true, as we have seen. But how much light does this form of truth shed upon the process of decline of this historical system, or on the existence of real historical alternatives to historical system based on the endless accumulation of capital? Therein lies the question.

This newer form of fundamental cultural resistance has a material base. The successive mobilizations of the world's anti-systemic movements have increasingly over time recruited elements economically and politically more marginal to the functioning of the system and less likely to profit, even eventually, from the accumulated surplus. At the same time, the successive demythologizations of these movements themselves have undermined the reproduction of universalist ideology within them, and the movements have thus begun to be open to more and more of these elements who have questioned ever more of their premises. Compared with the profile of the membership of the world's anti-systemic movements from 1850 to 1950, their profile from 1950 onwards contained more from peripheral zones, more women, more from 'minority' groups (however defined), and more of the work-force towards the unskilled, lowest-paid end of the scale. This was true both in the world as a whole and within all the states, both in the membership and in the leadership. Such a shift in social base could not but alter the cultural-ideological predilections of the world's anti-systemic movements.

We have tried thus far to describe how capitalism has in fact operated as a historical system. Historical systems however are just that—historical. They come into existence and eventually go out of existence, the consequence of internal processes in which the exacerbation of the internal contradictions lead to a structural crisis. Structural crises are massive, not momentary. They take time to play themselves out. Historical capitalism entered into its structural crisis in the early twentieth century and will probably see its demise as a historical system sometime in the next century. What will follow is hazardous to predict. What we can do now is analyze the dimensions of the structural crisis itself and try to preceive the directions in which the systemic crisis is taking us.

The first and probably most fundamental aspect of this crisis is that we are now close to the commodification of everything. That is, historical capitalism is in crisis precisely because, in pursuing the endless accumulation of capital, it is beginning to approximate that state of being Adam Smith asserted was 'natural' to man but which has *never* historically existed. The 'propensity [of humanity] to truck, barter, and exchange one thing for another' has entered into domains and zones previously untouched, and the pressure to expand commodification is relatively unchecked. Marx spoke of the market as being a 'veil' that hid the social relations of production. This was only true in the sense that, in comparison with direct local appropriation of surplus, indirect market (and therefore extra-local) appropriation of surplus was harder to discern and thus more difficult to combat politically for the world's work-force. The 'market' however operated in the quantitative terms of a general measure, money, and this clarified rather than mystified how much was actually being appropriated. What the accumulators of capital have counted on as a political safety-net is that only part of the labour has been so measured. Insofar as more and more labour is commodified, and householding becomes more and more a nexus of commodity relations, the flow of surplus becomes more and more visible. The political counterpressures thereby become more and more mobilized, and the structure of the economy more and more a direct target of the mobilization. The accumulators of capital, far from seeking to speed up proletarianization, try to retard it. But they cannot do so entirely, because of the contradictions of their own interests, being both individual entrepreneur and members of a class.

This is a steady, ceaseless process, impossible to contain as long as the economy driven by the endless accumulation of capital. The system may prolong its life by slowing down some of the activities which are wearing it out, but death always looms somewhere on the horizon.

One of the ways in which the accumulators of capital have prolonged the system is the political constraints they have built into it, which have forced anti-systemic movements along the paths of the creation of formal organizations using a strategy of seizure of state power. They had no real choice, but the strategy was a self-limiting one.

However, as we have seen, the contradictions of this strategy have themselves bred a crisis at the political level. This is not a crisis of the interstate system, which is still functioning very well in its primary mission to maintain hierarchy and contain opposition movements. The political crisis is the crisis of the anti-systemic movements themselves. As the distinction between socialist and nationalist movements begins to blur, and as more and more of these movements achieve state power (with all its limitations), the worldwide collectivity of movements has forced upon it a reassessment of all its pieties deriving from the original analyses of the nineteenth century. As the success of accumulators in accumulating has created too much commodification which threatens the system as such, so the success of the anti-systemic movements in seizing power has created too much reinforcement of the system which threatens to break through the acceptance by the world's work-forces of this self-limiting strategy.

Finally, the crisis is cultural. The crisis of the anti-systemic movements, the questioning of basic strategy, is leading to a questioning of the premisses of universalist ideology. This is going on in two arenas: the movements where the search for 'civilizational' alternatives is for the first time being taken seriously; and intellectual life, where the whole intellectual apparatus which came into being from the fourteenth century on is being slowly placed in doubt. In part, once again, this doubt is the product of its success. In the physical sciences, the internal processes of enquiry generated by modern scientific method seem to be leading to the questioning of the existing of the universal laws which were its premiss. Today there is talk of inserting 'temporality' into science. In the social sciences, a poor relation at one level, but the queen (that is, the culmination) of the sciences at another level, the whole developmentalist paradigm is today being explicity questioned at its heart.

The re-opening of intellectual issues is on the one hand therefore the product of internal success and internal contradictions. But it is also the product of the pressures of the movements, themselves in crisis, to be able to cope with, fight more effectively against, the structures of historical capitalism, whose crisis is the starting-point of all other activity.

The crisis of historical capitalism is often spoken of as the transition from capitalism to socialism. I agree with the formula, but it does not say much. We do not know yet how a socialist world order, one that radically narrows the gap of material well-being and disparity of real power between all persons, would operate. Existing states or movements which call themselves socialist offer little guide to the future. They are phenomena of the present, that is of the historical capitalist world-system, and must be evaluated within that framework. They may be agents of the demise of capitalism, though hardly uniformly so, as we have indicated. But the future world order will construct itself slowly, in ways we can barely imagine, never mind predict. It is therefore somewhat a leap of faith to believe that it will be good, or even better. But what we have we know has not been good, and as historical capitalism has proceeded on its historical path, it has in my view—by its very success—got worse, not better.

4.
Conclusion:
On Progress and
Transitions

If there is one idea which is associated with the modern world, is indeed its centrepiece, it is that of progress. That is not to say that everyone has believed in progress. In the great public ideological debate between conservatives and liberals, which partly preceded, but more especially followed, the French Revolution, the essence of the conservative position lay in doubt that the changes that Europe and the world were undergoing could be considered progress, or indeed that progress was a relevant and meaningful concept. Nevertheless, as we know, it was the liberals who heralded the age and incarnated what would become in the nineteenth century the dominant ideology of the long-existing capitalist world-economy.

It is not surprising that liberals believed in progress. The idea of progress justified the entire transition from feudalism to capitalism. It legitimated the breaking of the remaining opposition to the commodification of everything, and it tended to wipe away all the negatives of capitalism on the grounds that the benefits outweighed, by far, the harm. It is not at all surprising, therefore, that liberals believed in progress.

What is surprising is that their ideological opponents, the Marxists—the anti-liberals, the representatives of the oppressed working classes—believed in progress with at least as much passion as the liberals. No doubt, this belief served an important ideological purpose for them in turn. It justified the activities of the world socialist movement on the grounds that it incarnated the inevitable trend of historical development. Furthermore, it seemed very clever to propound this ideology, in that it purported to use the very ideas of bourgeois liberals to confound them.

There were unfortunately two minor shortcomings with the seemingly astute and certainly enthusiastic embrace of this secular faith in progress. While the idea of progress justified socialism, it justified capitalism too. One could hardly sing hosannas to the proletariat without offering prior praise to the bourgeoisie. Marx's famous writings on India offered ample evidence of this, but so indeed did the *Communist Manifesto*. Furthermore, the measure of progress being materialist (and could Marxists not assent to this?), the idea of progress could be turned, and has been turned in the past fifty years, against all the 'experiments in socialism'. Who has not heard the condemnations of the USSR on the grounds that its standard of living is below that of the USA? Furthermore, despite Krushchev's boasts, there is little reason to believe that this disparity will cease to exist fifty years from now.

The Marxist embrace of an evolutionary model of progress has been an enormous trap, which socialists have begun to suspect only recently, as one element in the ideological crisis that has been part of the overall structural crisis of the capitalist world-economy.

It is simply not true that capitalism as a historical system has represented progress over the various previous historical systems that it destroyed or transformed. Even as I write this, I feel the tremour that accompanies the sense of blasphemy. I fear the wrath of the gods, for I have been moulded in the same ideological forge as all my compeers and have worshipped at the same shrines.

One of the problems in analyzing progress is the one-sidedness of all measures proposed. It is said that scientific and technological progress is unquestionable and breathtaking, which is surely true, especially insofar as most technical knowledge is cumulative. But we never seriously discuss how much knowledge we have lost in the world-wide sweep of the ideology of universalism. Or if we do, we categorize such lost knowledge as mere (?) wisdom. Yet, at the simple technical levels of agricultural productivity and biological wholeness, we have been discovering of late that methods of human action discarded a century or two ago (a process enforced by enlightened elites upon backward masses) often need to be revived because they turn out to be more, not less, efficacious. More importantly, we are discovering at the very 'frontiers' of advanced science the tentative reinsertion of premises triumphantly discarded a century, or five centuries, ago.

It is said that historical capitalism has transformed the mechanical outreach of humanity. Each input of human energy has been rewarded with steadily greater outputs of products, which is surely true as well. But we do not calculate to what degree this has meant that humanity has reduced or increased the total inputs of energy that individuals separately, or all people within the capitalist world-economy collectively, have been called upon to invest, whether per unit of time or per lifetime. Can we be so sure that the world is less burdensome under historical capitalism than under prior systems? There is ample reason to doubt this, as is attested by the incorporation within our very superegos of the compulsion to work.

It is said that under no previous historical system did people live as comfortable a material life or have such a range of alternative life-experiences at their disposal as in this present system. Once again, this assertion rings true, is revealed by those comparison we regularly make with the lives of our immediate ancestors. Still, doubts in this domain have grown steadily throughout the twentieth century, as our now frequent references to 'quality of life' and mounting concern with anomie, alienation, and psychic maladies indicate. Finally it is said that historical capitalism has brought a massive increase in the margin of human safety—against hurt and death from endemic dangers (the four horsemen of the Apocalypse) and against erratic violence. Once again this is incontestable at a micro level (despite the recently rediscovered dangers of urban life). But has this really been true at a macro level, even up to now, and even omitting the Damoclean sword of nuclear war?

It is, let me say, at the very least by no means self-evident that there is more liberty, equality, and fraternity in the world today than there was one thousand years ago. One might arguably suggest that the opposite is true. I seek to paint no idyll of the worlds before historical capitalism. They were worlds of little liberty, little equality, and little fraternity. The only question is whether historical capitalism represented progress in these regards, or regression.

I do not speak of a measure of comparative cruelties. This would be hard to devise, lugubrious also, although there is little reason to be sanguine about the record of historical capitalism in this arena. The world of the twentieth century can lay claim to have exhibited some unusual talents of refinement in these ancient arts. Nor do I speak of the mounting and truly incredible social waste that has been the result of the competitive race for the endless accumulation of capital, a level of waste that may begin to border on the irreparable.

I rather wish to rest my case on material considerations, not those of the social future but those of the actual historical period of the capitalist world-economy. The argument is simple if audacious. I wish to defend the one Marxist proposition which even orthodox Marxists tend to bury in shame, the thesis of the absolute (not relative) immiseration of the proletariat.

I hear the friendly whispers. Surely you can't be serious; surely you mean relative immiseration? Is not the industrial worker strikingly better off today than in 1800? The industrial worker, yes, or at least many industrial workers. But industrial workers still comprise a relatively small part of the world's population. The overwhelming proportion of the world's work-forces, who live in rural zones or move between them and urban slums, are worse off than their ancestors five hundred years ago. They eat less well, and certainly have a less balanced diet. Although they are more likely to survive the first year of life (because of the effect of social hygiene undertaken to protect the privileged), I doubt that the life prospects of the majority of the world's population *as of age one* are greater than previously; I suspect the opposite is true. They unquestionably work harder—more hours per day, per year, per lifetime. And since they do this for less total reward, the rate of exploitation has escalated very sharply.

Are they politically and socially more oppressed or more exploited economically? This is harder to analyze. As Jack Goody once said, social science possesses no euphorimeters. The small communities within which most people led their lives in prior historical systems involved a form of social control which certainly constrained human choice and social variability. It no doubt appeared to many as a phenomenon of active oppression. The others, who were more satisfied, paid for their content with a narrow vision of human possibility.

The construction of historical capitalism has involved, as we all know, the steady diminution, even the total elimination, of the role of these small community structures. But what has taken their place? In many areas, and for long periods, the prior role of the community structures has been assumed by 'plantations', that is, by the oppressive control of large-scale politico-economic structures controlled by 'entrepreneurs'. The 'plantations' of the capitalist world-economy—whether based on slavery, imprisonment, share-cropping (forced or contractual), or wage-labour—can scarcely be said to have provided more leeway for 'individuality'. The 'plantations' can be considered an exceptionally effective mode of extracting surplus-value. No doubt they existed before in human history, but never before were they used as extensively for agricultural production—as distinct from mining and the construction of large-scale infrastructure, both of which, however, have tended to involve many fewer people in global terms.

Even where one form or another of direct authoritarian control of agricultural activity (what we have just labelled 'plantations') was not substituted for the prior laxer community structures of control, the disintegration of the community structures in rural zones was not experienced as a 'liberation', since it was inevitably accompanied, indeed frequently directly caused, by a constantly growing control by the emergent state structures which increasingly have been unwilling to leave the direct producer to his autonomous, local decision-making processes. The thrust has all been in the direction of forcing an increase in labour-input and in the specialization of this labour activity (which, from the point of view of the worker, weakened his negotiating position and increased his ennui).

Nor was this all. Historical capitalism developed an ideological framework of oppressive humiliation which had never previously existed, and which today we called sexism and racism. Let me be clear. Both the dominant position of men over women and generalized xenophobia were widespread, virtually universal, in prior historical systems, as we have already noted. But sexism was more than the dominant position of men over women, and racism more than generalized xenophobia.

Sexism was the relegation of women to the realm of non-productive labour, doubly humiliating in that the actual labour required of them was if anything intensified, and in that productive labour became in the capitalist world-economy, for the first time in human history, the basis of the legitimation of privilege. This set up a double bind which has been intractable within the system.

Racism was not hatred or oppression of a stranger, of someone outside the historical system. Quite the contrary, racism was the stratification of the work-force inside the historical system, whose object was to keep the oppressed groups inside the system, not expel them. It created the justification of low reward for productive labour, despite its primacy in the definition of the right to reward. It did this by defining work with the lowest remuneration as remuneration for the lowest-quality work. Since this was done *ex definitio*, no change in the quality of work could ever do more than change the form of the accusation, yet the ideology proclaimed the offer of a reward of individual mobility for individual effort. This double bind was equally intractable.

Both sexism and racism were social processes in which 'biology' defined position. Since biology was in any immediate sense unchangeable socially, we had seemingly a structure that was socially-created but was not amenable to social dismantling. This was of course not really so. What is true is that the structuring of sexism and racism could not and cannot be dismantled without dismantling the entire historical system which created them and which has been maintained in critical ways by their operation.

Hence, in both material and psychic terms (sexism and racism), there was absolute immiseration. This meant of course that there has been a growing 'gap' in the consumption of the surplus between the upper ten to fifteen per cent of the population in the capitalist world-economy and the rest. Our impression that this was not so has been based on three facts. First, the ideology of meritocracy has truly functioned to make possible considerable individual mobility, even the mobility of specific ethnic and/or occupational groups in the work-force. This occurred however without transforming fundamentally the overall statistics of the world-economy, since individual (or subgroup) mobility was countered by an increase in the size of the lower stratum, either by incorporating new populations into the world-economy or by differential demographic rates of growth.

The second reason why we haven't observed the growing gap is that our historical and social science analyses have concentrated on what has been happening within the 'middle classes'—that is, to that ten to fifteen per cent of the population of the world-economy who consumed more surplus than they themselves produced. *Within this sector* there really has been a relatively dramatic flattening of the curve between the very top (less than one per cent of the total population) and the truly 'middle' segments, or cadres (the rest of the ten to fifteen per cent). A good deal of the 'progressive' politics of the past several hundred years of historical capitalism has resulted in the steady diminution of the unequal distribution of world surplus-value among that small group who have shared in it. The shouts of triumph of this 'middle' sector over the reduction of their gap with the upper one per cent have masked the realities of the growing gap between them and the other eighty-five per cent .

Finally, there is a third reason why the phenomenon of the growing gap has not been central to our collective discussions. It is possible that, within the past ten to twenty years, under the pressure of the collective strength of the world's anti-systemic movements, and the approach to the economic asymptotes, there may have been a slowing down of absolute, though not of relative, polarization. Even this should be asserted with caution, and placed within the context of a five hundred years historical development of increased absolute polarization.

It is crucial to discuss the realities that have accompanied the ideology of progress because, unless we do that, we cannot intelligently approach the analysis of transitions from one historical system to another. The theory of evolutionary progress involved not merely the assumption that the later system was better than the earlier but also the assumption that some new dominant group replaced a prior dominant group. Hence, not only was capitalism progress over feudalism but this progress was essentially achieved by the triumph, the revolutionary triumph, of the 'bourgeoisie' over the 'landed aristocracy' (or 'feudal elements'). But if capitalism was not progressive, what is the meaning of the concept of the bourgeois revolution? Was there a single bourgeois revolution, or did it appear in multiple guises?

We have already argued that the image of historical capitalism having arisen via the overthrow of a backward aristocracy by a progressive bourgeoisie is wrong. Instead, the correct basic image is that historical capitalism was brought into existence by a landed aristocracy which transformed itself into a bourgeoisie because the old system was disintegrating. Rather than let the disintegration continue to uncertain ends, they engaged in radical structural surgery themselves in order to maintain *and significantly expand* their ability to exploit the direct producers.

If this new image is correct however, it radically amends our perception of the present transition from capitalism to socialism, from a capitalist world-economy to a social world-order. Up to now, the 'proletarian revolution' has been modelled, more or less, on the 'bourgeois revolution'. As the bourgeoisie overthrew the aristocracy, so the proletariat would overthrow the bourgeoisie. This analogy has been the fundamental building-block of the strategic action of the world socialist movement.

If there was no bourgeois revolution, does that mean there has been or will be no proletarian revolution? Not at all, logically or empirically. But it does mean we have to approach the subject of transitions differently. We need first to distinguish between change through disintegration and controlled change, what Samir Amin has called the distinction between 'decadence' and 'revolution', between the kind of 'decadence' which he asserts occurred with the fall of Rome (and is, he says, occurring now) and that more controlled change which occurred when going from feudalism to capitalism.

But this is not all. For the controlled changes (Amin's 're-volutions') need not be 'progressive', as we have just argued. Therefore, we must distinguish between the kind of structural transformation that would leave in place (even increase) the realities of the exploitation of labour, and one that would un-do this kind of exploitation or at least radically reduce it. What this means is that the political issue of our times is not whether there will be a transition from historical capitalism to something else. That is as certain as we can be about such things. The political issue of our times is whether this something else, the outcome of the transition, will be morally fundamentally different from what we have now, will be progress.

Progress is not inevitable. We are struggling for it. And the form the struggle is taking is not that of socialism versus capitalism, but that of a transition to a relatively classless society versus a transition to some new class-based mode of production (different from historical capitalism but not necessarily better).

The choice for the world bourgeoisie is not between maintaining historical capitalism and suicide. It is between on the one hand a 'conservative' stance, which would result in the continued disintegration of the system and its resultant transformation into an uncertain but probably more egalitarian world order; and, on the other hand, a bold attempt to seize control of the process of transition, in which the bourgeoisie itself would assume 'socialist' clothing, and seek to create thereby an alternative historical system which would leave intact the process of exploitation of the world's work-force, to the benefit of a minority.

It is in the light of these real political alternatives open to the world bourgeoisie that we should assess the history of both the world socialist movement and those states where socialist parties have come to power in one form or another.

The first and most important thing to remember in any such assessment is that the world socialist movement, indeed all forms of anti-systemic movements, as well as all revolutionary and/or socialist states, have themselves been integral products of historical capitalism. They were not structures external to the historical system but the excretion of processes internal to it. Hence they have reflected all the contradictions and constraints of the system. They could not and cannot do otherwise.

Their faults, their limitations, their negative effects are part of the balance-sheet of historical capitalism, not of a hypothetical historical system, of a socialist world-order, that does not yet exist. The intensity of the exploitation of labour in revolutionary and/or socialist states, the denial of political freedoms, the persistence of sexism and racism all have to do far more with the fact that these states continue to be located in peripheral and semi-peripheral zones of the capitalist world-economy than with the properties peculiar to a new social system. The few crumbs that have existed in historical capitalism for the working classes have always been concentrated in core areas. This is still disproportionately true.

The assessment of both the anti-systemic movements and the regimes which they have had a hand in creating cannot therefore be evaluated in terms of the 'good societies' they have or have not created. They can only be sensibly evaluated by asking how much they have contributed to the world-wide struggle to ensure that the transition from capitalism is towards an egalitarian socialist world-order. Here the accounting is necessarily more ambiguous, because of the workings of the contradictory processes themselves. All positive thrusts involve negative as well as positive consequences. Each weakening of the system in one way strengthens it in others. But not necessarily to equal degrees! The whole question is there.

There is no doubt that the greatest contribution of the anti-systemic movements has occurred in their mobilizing phases. Organizing rebellion, transforming consciousness, they have been liberating forces; and the contributions of individual movements here have become greater over time, through a feedback mechanism of historical learning.

Once such movements have assumed political power in state structures, they have done less well, because the pressures on them to mute their anti-systemic thrusts, from both without and within the movements, have increased geometrically. Nevertheless, this has not meant a totally negative balance-sheet for such 'reformism' and 'revisionism'. The movements in power have been to some extent the political prisoners of their ideology and hence subject to organized pressure from the direct producers within the revolutionary state and from the anti-systemic movements outside it.

The real danger occurs precisely now, as historical capitalism approaches its most complete unfolding—the further extension of the commodification of everything, the growing strength of the world family of anti-systemic movements, the continued rationalizing of human thought. It is this complete unfolding that will hasten the collapse of the historical system, which has thrived because its logic has hitherto been only partially realized. And precisely while and because it is collapsing, the bandwagon of the forces of transition will seem ever more attractive, and *therefore* the outcome will be ever less certain. The struggle for liberty, equality, and fraternity is protracted, comrades, and the locus of the struggle will be ever more inside the worldwide family of anti-systemic forces themselves.

Communism is Utopia, that is nowhere. It is the avatar of all our religious eschatologies: the coming of the Messiah, the second coming of Christ, nirvana. It is not a historical prospect, but a current mythology. Socialism, by contrast, is a realizable historical system which may one day be instituted in the world. There is no interest in a 'socialism' that claims to be a 'temporary' moment of transition towards Utopia. There is interest only in a concretely historical socialism, one that meets the minimum defining characteristics of a historical system that maximizes equality and equity, one that increases humanity's control over its own life (democracy), and liberates the imagination.

CAPITALIST CIVILIZATION

A Balance Sheet

The modern world–system, which is a capitalist world-economy, came into existence during the long sixteenth century in parts of Europe and the Americas, and has since expanded to include the entire globe. Historical capitalism has a number of characteristics unique to it as a historical system. One of them, one that has seldom received its due notice, is that it is a system which has been celebrated by some but vigorously denounced by others virtually from the outset. Indeed it was some three centuries into its development before the celebrators even began to seem numerous and outspoken. I cannot think of any other historical system that has been subjected to so much internal, and contradictory, evaluation by the mass of its participants as well as by its thinkers.

The idea that one can debate within the system the balance sheet of its virtues and vices, its positive and negative consequences—a debate I shall attempt to summarize—is probably unique to this system, and is in any case one of its defining features. Why this particular historical system alone should have given rise to this enduring public controversy is itself a question we shall want to explore.

The strangest part of the debate is that there are broadly speaking two sets of critics, and the two sets seem to contradict each other. One set of critics lambastes capitalism because it is too egalitarian, too disruptive of social peace and communal harmony. And the other set of critics finds historical capitalism to be, beneath a myth of the harmony of all interests, quintessentially inegalitarian.

One might be tempted to perceive such opposite criticisms as a sign that the proponents of capitalist civilization hold the strategic centre of moderation, against obviously extremist positions. One might be thus tempted, were this the argument that celebrators make. But they do not say this. Instead, in answer to those who argue the virtues of a hierarchical, harmonic social order, the advocates of historic capitalism have vaunted its revolutionary, progressive characteristics, said to be destructive of privilege. And to those critics who see capitalism as a system of inegalitarian, oppressive structures, its defenders have vaunted its ability to recognize and encourage what they call individual merit and asserted not only the desirability but also the inevitability of differential reward, of earned privilege, so to speak.

Thus the defenders of capitalism seem to be as self-contradictory as the opponents. Both critics and defenders, denouncers and celebrators, occupy the identical extreme positions, with no one (or virtually no one, it seems) to advocate the golden mean. This is a strange anomaly and one particularly strange in that it has been persistent. What purpose can it possibly serve for all the players to put themselves in such a confused line-up? It is as though there were two sports teams which wore the same uniforms and milled around in the same arena in very mixed-up formations.

In this case, can there be a score? Can there be a balance sheet? I do not even ask, can there be an impartial balance sheet, but can there be one at all? I think that we will not be able to address this question until we sort out why and how it is possible that such a confused struggle has been sustained.

The Four Horsemen of the Apocalypse, or Basic Needs

Over the past 5,000 years, humanity has developed an array of religions, all of which have shared at least one basic feature. They have attempted to give some response to, some solace for, the perceived material miseries of the world. These are summarised quite well in the Christian imagery of the Four Horsemen of the Apocalypse. The four are war (that is, war between peoples or states); civil war; famine; and death by pestilence, plague, or wild beasts. These Four Horsemen are the horrors of the world, the disrupters of peace, pleasure, and satisfaction.

The religions of the world offered whatever solace they could, but they did so on the premise that there existed no political (that is, no worldly) solution to these evils. The evils were inevitable, unless and until there were a messianic era (at least in the case of some religions), or some other way of getting beyond history.

Capitalist civilization was extraordinary in that it laid claim to being able to get 'beyond history' within history, to resolve the dilemmas of inevitable evils, to create the kingdom of God upon earth, in short, to overcome the menace of the Four Horsemen of the Apocalypse. From the beginning, the celebrators have argued that capitalism as a historical system would, at the very least, meet the 'basic needs' (to use the terminology of recent decades) of all persons living within its bounds.

The argument was in a sense quite simple and straightforward. Capitalism, by increasing the efficiency of production, has increased collective wealth vastly. Even if this wealth has been unequally distributed, there has been enough to ensure that everyone received more than the level possible under other and previous historical systems. This has been called the 'trickle down' theory of distribution, itself merely the specification of the 'invisible hand' theory of production. It is because of these presumed beneficial consequences that the proponents of capitalist civilization not merely have argued that a capitalist system is distinctive from and better than all others but also have simultaneously claimed that it is the only 'natural' system.

What evidence have these proponents offered for these views? Fundamentally, the evidence has been demonstrative. Look, they say, at the modern world. Is it not richer than any other known world? Have not technological achievements been fabulous? Is everyone not in some real sense better off? And, in particular, is it not the case that those countries where capitalism seems to be accepted and practised most fully are precisely the countries that are the wealthiest and the most economically advanced?

This argument from demonstration has been, for some two hundred years now, an extremely persuasive one to very large numbers of persons and should therefore be taken quite seriously. It is based very heavily on the central role of applied science within historical capitalism. Once again using the evidence of demonstration, it is argued that only within the framework of historical capitalism have science and technology truly flourished, since it is only within this system that scientists have been released from the constraints imposed upon them by previous systems. And this in turn has been true because the direct and indirect subsidy of scientific activity by entrepreneurs was ultimately materially very rewarding to these entrepreneurs. Let us try to evaluate the plausibility of the arguments in terms of each of the Four Horsemen, taken in reverse order.

Has capitalist civilization postponed (it obviously could not totally eliminate) death by pestilence, plague, and wild beasts? This is the question of health and sanitation in its broadest sense. In the fourteenth century, the Eurasian landmass suffered from the Black Death. Our imperfect estimates suggest that about one-third of the population in affected zones died premature deaths because of it.

This was undoubtedly not the first such pandemic in the history of the world, but it seems to have been the last known one of such extensiveness. Why? Two reasons basically. The first is safeguarding the individual. Medical knowledge has advanced to such an extent that we have learned better both how to avert the onset of such diseases (e.g., by inoculation) and how to minimize their impact once they have been contracted by individuals. The second reason is safeguarding the collectivity. We have learned how to create a better public health environment as well as techniques to contain the spread of disease. (One of the earliest and more primitive of such techniques was the quarantine, a word that is derived from the forty-day isolation period imposed on persons arriving in the port of Ragusa during the Black Death.)

Is there any other kind of demonstrative evidence to put into the balance sheet? There are at least three phenomena which move in the opposite direction. First, there were the devastating consequences of the mixing of parasitic gene pools because of precisely the technological advances in transport that were part and parcel of the expansion of a capitalist world economy. This has been most clearly studied in the case of the transoceanic exchanges between 1500 and 1700. Very large proportions of the populations indigenous to the Americas—far more than a third—were wiped out in this process. Similar phenomena occurred in Oceania and the remoter zones of Africa, Asia, and Europe.

Secondly, medical research of only the last two decades is making clear how many diseases have actually expanded in number due to environmental changes directly linked to the economic technologies that have been part and parcel of capitalist civilization. Thirdly, it is quite possible that wholly new disease patterns are emerging out of and, in some sense, because of, the dramatic demographic expansion throughout the globe. There is some suggestion that this may be a major factor in the new AIDS epidemic (as well as that of other auto-immune diseases). We may thus be at the threshold of new dramatic plagues of a different kind.

How do we compare the number of lives 'extended' through medical advances against the number of lives 'never created' because of sudden parasitic exchanges? The latter in particular is difficult to quantify, and thus there is no very good way to make this comparison for the moment. But we should note at least the assessment is not simple and surely not one-sided. It is clear that infant mortality has declined significantly in the more industrial-ized states of the world-system. It seems to have declined in the South as well in the twentieth century, although whether this is true in periods of stagnation in the world-economy or only true of the periods of expansion is less clear. We know that, in the industrialized countries, those aged sixty or older have a greater ability to survive ailments than previously because of advances in medical technology. These two changes—decline of infant mortality and extension of life for those who have reached sixty years—account for a large part, even perhaps all, of the increased average longevity. Whether those who have survived infancy are more likely to reach sixty years of age than previously is far less clear. Whether new plagues will change even the overall figures is certainly unclear. But we can tentatively credit capitalist civiliza-tion with a positive, if very geographically uneven, record in the struggle against disease.

What of the struggle against hunger? Is famine less of a threat today than in times past? In the pre-modern era, the main problem for humanity was short-run weather shifts which affected production annually. Given the weakness of transport systems, the limited amount of long-term food storage, and the widespread rarity of individual money reserves, any significant diminution of local supply of staple foods caused immediate grave problems. It is largely the case today that technological advances have sheltered many (perhaps most) parts of the world from the predictable vagaries of the short-term weather.

But what of the medium-term shifts in environmental conditions? The very same technological advances that have allowed us to intrude upon natural biospherical conditions in the short run have upset biospherical conditions in the medium run. The evisceration of forests, the desertification of savannah zones all involve continuing destruction of peoples and their long-term food supply. We are as yet unable to assess fully the damage from chemico-biological pollution, so accentuated in the twentieth century. If the ozone layer is further depleted, the destruction of lives (directly, and through its impact on the food supply) may be enormous.

So, on the one hand, there has been a remarkable expansion of the total production and productivity of food production, and on the other hand an extraordinarily skewed distribution system, substituting medium-run threats for short-term threats for the majority of the world's population, particularly the 50 to 80 per cent at the bottom.

What of civil war? Has it decreased? I include in this category all violence between groups that is not formally a war between two geographically distinct states or peoples or a rebellion of a conquered territory against an imperial ruler. In a sense, one could argue that 'civil war' is an invention of the capitalist world-economy. It is the product of the complex relationship between the construct 'people' and the construct 'state' in a system whereby there is an extremely high degree of admixture and propinquity in urban zones of groups defined socially as different 'peoples'. This is not accidental, but is derived from the intrinsic structuring of the capitalist world-economy.

The capitalist world-economy has required for its optimal

functioning widespread and continuous migrations of people (both forced and voluntary) in order to fulfil labour-force needs at particular geographical locations. Along with this has gone an ethnicization of the world's work force, such that in any given locale, the population is seen as divided into various ethnic groupings (whether the marker of such ethnicity is perceived skin colour, language, religion, or some other cultural construct). There tends to be at all times a high correlation of households between their ethnic stratum (as defined locally) and their occupational and class location. Of course, the details constantly change—the definition of ethnic boundaries, which ethnic group correlates with which occupational stratum—but the stratification principle is an enduring feature of the capitalist world-economy, serving both to reduce overall costs of labour and to contain thrusts to delegitimize the state structures.

This process of ethnicization has a clear downside in terms of any balance sheet. It creates the structural foundation of continuous struggle both between upper and lower ethnic strata, and among ethnic strata at the lower level. These struggles tend to become more acute each time there is a cyclical downturn in the world-economy, which is half the historical time. The struggles have frequently deteriorated into violent forms, from minor riots to wholesale genocides.

The crucial element is that the ethnicization of the world's work force has required an ideology of racism, in which large segments of the world's population have been defined as under classes, as inferior beings, and therefore as deserving ultimately of whatever fate comes their way out of the immediate political and social struggles. These 'civil wars' have not grown fewer with time but, if anything, have become more oppressive and deadly in the twentieth century. This is a very large minus in the balance sheet of our current world-system.

Finally, there is war itself. Wars between states and/or peoples seem to have existed under all historical systems for as long as we have some recorded evidence. War is quite clearly not a phenomenon particular to the modern world-system. On the other hand, once again the technological achievements of capitalist civilization serve as much ill as good. One bomb in Hiroshima killed more people than whole wars in pre-modern times. Alexander the Great in his whole sweep of the Middle East could not compare in destructiveness to the impact of the Gulf War on Iraq and Kuwait.

Finally, we must take into full account the material polarization of the world-system. The total material wealth has grown immensely, if we mean by material wealth all commodified and commodifiable objects, even if this economic 'growth' has been at the cost of largely exhausting some primary natural materials. And this surplus-value has been distributed amongst a far larger percentage of the population than in any previous historical system. Before 1500, in the various historical systems that existed, there was almost always a rich or richer stratum. But, before 1500, this stratum was extremely small in size. Symbolically we may refer to one per cent of the population, though in some cases the percentage may have been larger.

In capitalist civilization, the number of persons who have shared in the surplus-value has been much larger. This is the group referred to as the middle classes. They are a significant stratum. But it would be quite in error to exaggerate their size. This group, worldwide, has probably never exceeded one-seventh of the world's population. To be sure, many of these 'middle strata' are concentrated in certain geographical zones, and thus, in the core countries of the capitalist world-economy, they may be a majority of the citizenry. Indeed, the high concentration of middle strata within the political boundaries of one state is today a defining feature of core zones. But worldwide the percentage is far lower. Perhaps as much as 85 per cent of the people who live within the structures of the capitalist world-economy are clearly not living at standards higher than the world's working populations of 500 to 1,000 years ago. Indeed, it could be argued that many, even most, of them are materially worse off. In any case, they certainly work much harder in order merely to scrape by; they may eat less, but they surely buy more.

Has then capitalist civilization defeated the Four Horsemen of the Apocalypse? At most, only partially and even then very unevenly. Thus far, however, we have only discussed the question quantitatively. We must discuss it qualitatively as well. These are all the issues usually debated under the rubric 'quality of life'.

The Quality of Individual Life

The first issue is the quality of material life. This has to do with comfort and with variety of consumption beyond the 'basic needs' of survival. Here too the picture is mixed. Our 'consumer society' of the twentieth century is to be sure a function of science and its gadgetry. We have mechanisms undreamt of in previous civilizations: electricity, telephones, radios and television, indoor plumbing, refrigerators and air conditioners, automobiles, to name only the most obvious and today the most widespread. In 1500, even a book was an extraordinary luxury.

Once again, however, we also know that distribution is extraordinarily uneven. Most American families have a car; exceedingly few Chinese or Indian families do, although most of them may have access to a radio, if only as the collective property of a village. At an absolute level, even the poorest strata probably have more of these gadgets than did their ancestors, even if the relative gap between the bottom and the top is not merely immense but growing. It is not, however, even sure that the absolute curve is a linear upward one. We may well have reached the top of the curve for the bottom 50 to 80 per cent, and face the possibility that the absolute curve for them may turn down again.

The situation is even starker when we turn to one of the most remarkable inventions of capitalist civilization, tourism. In no previous historical system did there exist the concept that people, even wealthy and powerful people, would spend a part of their lifetime exempt from income-producing work in order to travel, observe, and enjoy pleasures that were not part of their ordinary ongoing life pattern. What originated in early modern times as the sport of a handful of aristocrats has become in the late twentieth century the normal expectation of the world's middle strata. This has of course been made possible by the same technological advances. But note two things. At the very most, 5 to 10 per cent of the world's population can engage even once in a tourist expedition. But also, even this amount has put such a strain on the intrinsic possibilities of bearing the burden of tourist depredation that the very existence of the highest-quality objects of tourism are in peril. Tourism is deeply destructive if there is an overload. There is today already an overload, and that at a point where 80 per cent of the world's population are still excluded from participation. If the numbers were to expand, safeguarding tourist sites could only be handled by some kind of formal rationing system, at which point, at the level of the individual, the benefits would decline markedly.

The debate about the comfort and variety of individual material satisfactions is one major source of contrary evaluations. The critics of capitalist civilization point to the gaping differential between what is available to one-seventh of the world's population and life as it is lived in the urban slums and rural poverty zones of the world. The contrast is dramatic, even terrifying. The defenders of capitalist civilization argue that the gap is only relative, and that in absolute terms the world's poor are less poor than 500 years ago. The evidence on the absolute gap is, I have suggested, itself a subject of empirical debate. The moral question is whether even a growing gap that is only relative is acceptable. The response of the defenders is to argue that the gap no longer seems to be growing and may soon diminish.

Defenders of capitalist civilization argue further that, even if the picture on individual comfort and variety of consumption is mixed, one unalloyed benefit of capitalist civilization has been the creation and geometric expansion of the world's educational institutions. This expansion has had the effect, they argue, of permitting all individuals to realize better their potential and some individuals to cross class barriers by demonstrating their abilities.

The very concept of universal formal education is a product (and a relatively late product) of the capitalist world-economy. Educational institutions have steadily expanded in both the length of time students spend in school and how accessible schools are to divers groups in the world's population. This expansion has been going on for some two centuries now, but was particularly accelerated in the post-1945 period. Today there is virtually no political jurisdiction in which primary education is not available, at least in theory, to all male children, and in most to all female children as well. There has been a simultaneous expansion (albeit a lesser one) of secondary and tertiary education.

It is said that increased education means increased access to higher levels of full-time employment. Of course, this is true as a relative matter. That is to say, there is a high correlation between years of education and earned income. But as an absolute assertion, it is very dubious. The expansion of educational facilities has led directly to an escalation of educational prerequisites for given employments. Hence, the person who has completed a primary school education in 1990 may be eligible for the exact same job that a person with no formal education obtained in 1890.

One important consequence of burgeoning educational institutions has been the removal of whole age cohorts during daytime hours both from the household and from workplaces outside the home. Whole age cohorts no longer earn income for their households but, on the contrary, cost the households significant amounts of revenue even if there is no school tuition. Thus, the households are mandated to invest in what has been somewhat grandiosely designated as 'human capital'. Do the benefits exceed the costs for most households in the world-system?

A second major consequence of universal education has been the development and anchoring of the concept and individual reality of multiple 'stages of life'. In previous historical systems, a person's life was one long period of work and social participation, bracketed on each side with a short period of total dependency at the outset and a short period (if one at all) of relatively high dependency on the tail end. Now, we pass a relatively long period as partially dependent children outside the work force. This long childhood has come to be divided into units corresponding with the school system: early childhood for nursery schools, true childhood for elementary school, adolescence for secondary school, and late adolescence for university education, now being supplemented by young adulthood for advanced university training and/or first years of full-time work. This story then continues for further age groupings: mature adulthood, the third age, and now even the fourth age. The content of role allocation during mature adulthood has of course tended to be different for women than for men.

The great plus in this social differentiation of multiple life segments is said to be the specialized attention and adjustment it makes possible in terms of human fulfilment. No doubt this is true up to a certain point. But it should be noted that this plus comes with a reasonably large minus: the exclusion from full paticipation in power and material benefits of all those outside the now far narrower range of years defining male mature adulthood. Under the umbrella of egalitarian common passages through life's stages, we have erected a quite rigid curvilinear age hierarchy which is probably more consequential than the less complex age hierarchies of previous historical systems.

The ultimate question is, nonetheless, whether and to what degree the education is educational, that is, to revert to its etymological origins, how much education has 'led people out of' (*educere*) narrower horizons to wider ones. The basic assumption is that local, home-based socialization into knowledge and values is intrinsically parochial, but that formal education offers literacy, numeracy, empirical knowledge, and analytic skills which permit its recipients to transcend their parochial limitations and share in some universalist awareness of human potential in general and their own in particular.

However, for as long as there has been widespread formal education, there have been critics who have asserted the 'failures' of each and every particular local or national variety. The critics have always argued that exactly this function of 'leading people out of' parochial vision towards some larger vision (some call it truth, others call it sensitivity to diversity) has not in fact occurred. How strong a case can be made that it has in fact occurred? Education has certainly not reduced the phenomenon of 'civil war'; it may indeed have enhanced it; it may even be its principal source of nourishment. The greater fulfilment of individual potential, to the degree that it has occurred, may well be the consequence as much of increased geographical mobility as of increased education. Most parents see education as an urgent economic necessity for their children, running very fast to keep up with the continuing escalation of formal educational requirements for job allocation.

But most persons attending school see school as a burden and an exclusion from the work world. Are we absolutely certain that the appreciation of the children is so irrational?

The Quality of Collective Life

There are two supreme virtues in the construction of our social life that the advocates of capitalist civilization claim as its accomplishment, or at least its promise: universalism, and democracy. Yet once again, the critics argue precisely the opposite. They point to the absence of these same two phenomena as the supreme vice in capitalist civilization. As in other parts of the balance sheet, a judgment depends on whom and what one is measuring. What is universalism? It has many domains. Universalism is the argument that there are truths that are rational, objective, and eternal—hence universal. Today we call this science. Universalism is also the argument that there exists some sort of natural law that determines a universal ethic, and consequently some social practices which all should accept and follow. Today we call this human rights. Universalism is, as well, the belief that there exist objective standards of competence that determine appropriate allocations of positions in the work force. Today we call this meritocracy. It is this universalist trio of science, human rights, and meritocracy that is the pride of the advocates of capitalist civilization. One can see why there is such an emphasis on science, why science has become a virtual secular religion, with its truths revealed to mere mortals by its priests who alone have true access to universal knowledge. For modern science is the underpinning of modern technology, and it is modern technology that is credited with the presumed achievement that the world today both meets the basic needs of mankind and has heightened the quality of individual life. This faith in science reflects (reflects, rather than is the basis of) the confidence in the endlessly expanding possibilities of capitalist accumulation.

The vision of science as the relentless march towards the formulation of universal laws, what we may call the Baconian-Newtonian vision of science, has been the dominant vision for some 500 years now. But, beginning in the late nineteenth century, and with considerably growing strength in the last twenty years, this vision of science has come under severe challenge within the scientific community itself. This has taken the form of the 'new science' with its concepts of the normality both of chaos and of open systems far from equilibrium, as well as the pervasiveness of dissipative structures leading to bifurcations going in inherently unpredictable (but nonetheless orderly) directions.

The basic question that the 'new science' raises for our balance sheet is the issue of what scientific questions have not been asked for 500 years, which scientific risks have not been pursued. It raises the question of who has decided what scientific risks were worth taking, and what have been the consequences in terms of the power structures of the world. One wonders, for example, if our present ecological dilemmas, the direct result of the externalization of costs by capitalist entrepreneurs, would not have been at least lessened, if not altogether avoided, by a more holistic scientific approach that would have made the study of dissipative structures and inevitable bifurcations central to its analysis, rather than by one that relegated such systemic dilemmas to the category of external obstacles inherently capable of a technical solution, while presuming that the linear trends in place would simply continue.

To ask the question is to answer it, since it suggests that so-called universalist science has been both constricted and particularist while asserting the contrary. If then we are to make a balance sheet of its achievements, we must measure not merely the technology it has permitted to be created, but the alternatives that were missed or failed to be pursued. We must recite not merely the credit but the blame. The next thirty years of scientific activity may permit us to have a more sober evaluation of the last 500.

If not truth, then at least freedom? Has not capitalist civilization offered the world the first flourishing of a universalizing model of freedom? Is not the very concept of the legal and moral priority of human rights an invention of the modern world? No doubt it is. The language of intrinsic human rights represented a significant advance beyond the previous language of world religions in terms of its universal applicability and its thisworldliness. Capitalist civilization may well be credited with legitimating such language and of furthering its spread.

And yet we know that human rights are sorely lacking in the real practices of the world. It is true that in previous historical systems there was very little pretence to human rights. Today all political entities claim to be its defenders. But Amnesty International finds no difficulty in drawing up long lists of its violation everywhere on the globe. Is the proclamation of human rights more than the hypocritical homage vice pays to virtue?

One argument may be that human rights are better observed in some parts of the world-system than in others. No doubt this is true, albeit even in the countries where it is apparently less of a problem, there are still entire internal zones and strata of the population whose human rights are regularly violated. And the world's migrants, who are an increasing and not a decreasing proportion of the world's population in our present world-system, are notoriously deprived of such human rights.

But even if we acknowledge that we can show a range of observance of human rights such that there are better and worse locales, what does this then prove? For it is easy to see there exists a correlation between richer and more powerful states and fewer (or less obvious) violations, and of poorer and weaker states and grosser violations. One can use this correlation in two opposite ways. For some it proves that the more 'capitalist' the state, the more the acceptance of human rights, and of course then vice versa. But to others it proves in one more way the concentration of advantages in one zone of the world-system, and the concentration of negative effects in the other, itself seen as the outcome of historical capitalism, in which human rights are precisely not a universal value but a reward of privilege.

With both universal science and universal human rights coming into question, the advocates often turn to their strongest claim, universalist allocation of position, or meritocracy. In the mythology of capitalist civilization, in all prior historical systems, individuals were born to their position; in historical capitalism alone there is said to be allocation by merit—the 'career open to talents' proclaimed by the French Revolution.

Once again we must be careful to compare myth and reality. It is not true that individual social advancement was unknown in previous historical systems. It always existed. Else, how could we have had the constant turnover of aristocracies, largely via military prowess, that was pervasive everywhere? And religious structures also always incorporated social ascent by merit, in their case by non-military prowess. Indeed, even ascent via the market was widespread if not commonplace.

What is different in capitalist civilization has been two things. First, the process of meritocracy has been proclaimed as an official virtue instead of being merely a *de facto* reality. The culture has been different. And secondly, the percentage of the world's population for whom such ascent was possible has gone up. But even though it has gone up, meritocratic ascent remains very much the attribute of a minority. For meritocracy is a false universalism. It proclaims a universal opportunity that, by definition, is only meaningful if it is not universal. Meritocracy is intrinsically elitist.

Furthermore, we must investigate the degree to which the institutions that translate meritocracy into practice make their decisions in fact on grounds of merit. This brings us back to the question of the operations of educational structures. Do they indeed perform a perfect triage on the basis of merit? Of course, they are able to quantify merit in terms of scores. But since the scoring is done locally by locals according to locally chosen criteria, these scores are doubtfully comparable. What is probably the most that can be said for meritocratic scoring is that it can easily distinguish the small group of quite exceptional persons and that of quite incompetent persons, leaving a very large group in between among whom the scoring process does not allow us to choose in reliable ways. In terms however of a job structure that needs at most a quarter of the 80 per cent in the middle competency group in higher paying positions, choices must be made, and there is clear evidence that here the criterion of family social position intrudes in a major way. The institutionalized meritocratic system helps a few to gain access to positions they merit and from which they might otherwise be barred. But it allows many more to gain access to positions on the basis of ascribed status under the cover of having gained this access by achievement.

The second main claim to virtue of capitalist civilization has been that it has nourished democracy and made it flourish. Let us define democracy quite simply as the maximization of participation in decision-making at all levels on the basis of equality. Thus, 'one person one vote' has become one symbol of a democratic state structure, even if it alone is merely a first step in democratic participation. The basic drive for democracy is an egalitarian drive. The counter-drives are two: the drive for privilege, and the drive for competent performance. Both counter-drives result in hierarchies.

The existence of two counter-drives rather than one explains the profound gulf in the interpretation of reality. The defenders of capitalist civilization argue that it has been the first historical system to have ended the hierarchy of privilege. Of course, they add, the hierarchy of competent performance has been and has had to be maintained. For example, an infant cannot be permitted to have equal say with the parent. The critics of capitalist civilization charge a vast deception. They assert that the hierarchy of privilege masquerades as the hierarchy of competent performance, and that the hierarchy that may be legitimate in a limited range of social situaions (the issue of the social autonomy of the infant) is widely and inappropriately applied to a far wider range of situations in work and the community where in fact democratic (that is, egalitarian) norms should prevail. Here we see the link between the debate about meritocracy and the debate about democracy.

If we are to draw up a balance sheet of historical capitalism, we must take into account the totality of social arenas that exist in the world-system, evaluate each in terms of the degree to which a hierarchy of decision-making is or is not truly justified in terms of the needs of competent performance (as opposed to those of privilege), and summarize these evaluations for our current world-system in comparison with parallel summary evaluations of previous historical systems. This is a daunting task. The principal argument in favour of the thesis of greater democracy within historical capitalism has been the spread of political voting systems. To be sure, on the other side, skepticism is frequently expressed about the substantive significance of formal suffrage. But even leaving this aside, the principal argument against the thesis of democratization via capitalist civilization has been the decline of communitarian institutions in the modern world simultaneous with the rise of voting systems. What was gained in the one arena, it is asserted, was more than lost in the other.

This brings us to the discussion of alienation. It is at this point that conservative and radical critics of capitalist civilization join forces. Alienation is the opposite of fulfilment of potential, the already noted claim about the virtue of formal education. Alienation refers to ways in which we become alien from ourselves, our 'true nature', indeed our potential. Both the conservative and the radical critiques of capitalist civilization have centred on the degree to which commodification, in particular but not only of labour-power, is profoundly dehumanizing.

For the defenders of capitalist civilization, this is mysticism which cannot compare with the real material benefits of the modern world. They challenge whether it is possible in any significant way to operationalize the concept of alienation. For the critics, however, it seems easy to concretize. They point to the multiple forms of profound psychic and socio-psychological malaise of the modern world. Once again our measurements are weak. We know the madnesses of our own historical system. We have some weak idea of the madnesses that were known in other historical systems. We are ill equipped to compare them. We can nonetheless assert three things. One, the madnesses, or if you will the forms of malaise, of our system are extensive. Two, a case can be made for some clear linkages between these psychic problems and the specific social structures of our historical system. Three, if anything, the extensiveness of these psychic problems seems to have increased within our system as time has gone on. This last may perhaps be merely the outcome of closer social monitoring of reality—for example, of random urban violence. But some part of the perceived increase seems to be subject to solid measurement—for example, the addictions to drugs.

Nor must we forget trees. The natural beauties of the physical world are part of what creates human pleasure. Commodification has led, inevitably, to a wholesale destruction of these natural beauties. To be sure, other beauties have been constructed. Perhaps they are better. But the alternative beauties are themselves commodified, and hence less democratically available to the viewers than were trees. The artificial beauties are available primarily to a minority.

Cui Bonō, and Why a Debate?

We can now turn to the balance sheet. Yes, it is possible to argue one, at least a qualitative one. It is clear from this review of the arguments that the picture is not one-sided. Is there however some underlying thread which can summarize the pros and cons? I think there is. I start with the assumption that all known historical systems have been systems that incarnated a hierarchy of privilege. There never was a golden era. The question is thus a choice not between good and bad historical systems, but between better and worse. Has capitalist civilization been better or worse than prior historical systems? (I leave aside for the moment whether future ones could be better or worse, or will probably be better or worse.)

It seems to me the only pertinent question is: *cui bonō*? It is clear that the size of the privileged strata as a percentage of the whole has grown significantly under historical capitalism. And for these people, the world they know is better on the whole than any their earlier counterparts knew. They are certainly better off materially and in terms of health, life opportunities, and freedom from arbitrary constraints imposed by small ruling groups. Whether they are better off psychically is open to much question, but perhaps they are no worse off.

But for the other end of the spectrum, the 50 to 85 per cent of the world's population who are not the recipients of privilege, the world they know is almost certainly worse than any their earlier counterparts knew. It is likely they are worse off materially, despite the technological changes. In substantive as opposed to formal terms, they are more, not less, subject to arbitrary constraints, since the central mechanisms are more pervasive and more efficient. And they bear the brunt of the various kinds of psychic malaise, as well as of the destructiveness of 'civil wars'.

The world of capitalist civilization is a polarized and a polarizing world. How then has it survived this long? This is where the public debate over the balance sheet has come in. What has preserved the system thus far has been the hope of incremental reformism, the eventual bridging of the gap. The debate has itself fed this hope doubly. The assertion of the virtues has served to persuade many of the long-term benefits of the system. And the discussion of the vices has made many feel that they could thereby organize effectively to bring about political transformation. Capitalist civilization has not only been a successful civilization. It has above all been a seductive one. It has seduced even its victims and its opponents.

But if you believe, as I do, that all historical systems without exception have limited lives and must eventually give way to other successor systems, you must assume that our world-system cannot be stable forever. It is to this theme, the future prospects of capitalist civilization, that we shall next turn.

Future Prospects

Capitalist civilization has reached the autumn of its existence. Autumn, as we know, is a wonderful season, at least in the regions where capitalist civilization was born. Past the first bloom of spring, past the full richness of summer, we reap the harvest in autumn. But in autumn it is also true that the leaves fall from the trees. And whilst we know that there is much to enjoy in autumn, we know also that we must prepare for the winter frost, the end of the cycle, the end too of a historical system.

If we wish to understand how a system approaches its end, we must look at its contradictions, since all historical systems (indeed all systems) have inbuilt contradictions, which is why they all have limited lives. I shall discuss three basic contradictions whose increasing strain determine the future prospects of historical capitalism. They are the dilemma of accumulation, the dilemma of political legitimization, and the dilemma of the geocultural agenda. Each dilemma has been with us from the beginning of the system; each has been approaching the threshold of the point where the contradiction can no longer be contained, that is, the point at which the necessary adjustments to maintain the normal functioning of the system will have so high a cost that they cannot bring the system into temporary equilibrium.

The Dilemma of Accumulation

The endless accumulation of capital is the raison d'être and the central activity of capitalist civilization. We have already seen, in reviewing the balance sheet, that its successful accomplishment is one of its boasts and one of its justifications. But what is its contradiction, its dilemma?

The basic strain is that maximizing profits and therefore accumulation requires achieving relative monopolies of production. The greater the degree of monopolization, the greater the possibility of obtaining a wide gap between total production costs and effective sales prices. Therefore, all capitalists seek to monopolize. However, high profits are attractive, and others will always seek to enter the markets where they can be made. Hence, monopolies invite competition, which undermines monopolies and high profits simultaneously. But each time the sources of high profits are debilitated, capitalists (singly and collectively) search for new sources of high profits, that is, new ways to monopolize sectors of production. This tension between the need to monopolize and its self-destructive character explains the cyclical nature of capitalist economic activity, and accounts for the underlying axial division of labour between core products (highly monopolized) and peripheral products (highly competitive) in a capitalist world-economy.

Economic monopolies are never achieved in the market. Markets are inherently anti-monopolistic. The advantage of one producer over others is always temporary, since other producers always can and will copy the elements that gave one producer the advantage. This is dictated by the need of all producers to survive in the struggle to be a locus of accumulation. Since, however, significant accumulation is never possible for long via market mechanisms, all producers must look beyond the market to permit them to succeed. They look to two institutions: the state, which is quite concrete as an institution; and 'custom', which is quite amorphous but nonetheless real as an institution.

What can states do for producers? Two things essentially. They can create conditions that lead to the monopolization of sales. And they can create conditions that lead to the monopsonization of purchases of the factors of production. The simplest way to do this is by formal legislation. But formal legislation has two constraints. One is that it applies only within the frontiers of the state that is legislating, whereas the real market exists within the world-economy as a whole. The second is that the state is subject to many political pressures against such legislation—from entrepreneurs who are left out, and from all those non-producer groups whose economic position is hurt by such legislation. For these reasons, the full legislative route has seldom been followed. When it has, as in the case of the so-called (now mostly former) socialist states, it has revealed its inefficacy as a mechanism of long-term accumulation of capital. The route that has been more usual is the selective, and often indirect, intrusion of states into the market. They intrude first of all as states vis-à-vis other states, and especially as strong states vis-à-vis weaker states, imposing preferential access, and most importantly, preventing denial of access to markets in the weaker countries while simultaneously making it difficult for competitors in weaker countries to copy efficiencies. They intrude secondly through their budgetary, fiscal, and redistributive decisions designed to favour some sets of producers against any and all competition. They intrude thirdly by preventing sellers of factors of production (especially, of labour-power) from combating the monopsonistic positions of certain sets of producers.

The specific acts of states vary constantly, because world market conditions constantly change, the balance of power in the interstate system constantly changes, and the internal political situation within states constantly changes. The attitude of sets of producers towards their own state therefore constantly changes as well, as the likelihood that state action will help or hurt them in particular changes. But what is constant is the search by some powerful producers for state enhancement of their market position, and the largely positive response of the states to such demands. Had this not been a constant of the capitalist world-economy, capitalist civilization would never have flourished.

Producers have not however relied only on the state. They have relied also on 'custom'. As I noted, this is amorphous but not thereby insignificant. Custom includes the creation of markets via the creation of tastes. Advertising and marketing are obvious constructions of custom but they are only a small part of this story. A far larger part is the shaping of the entire value system as fostered and reproduced by all the institutions of socialization created and refined over 500 years of modern history. It is to this vast framework we point when we speak of the existence of the 'consumer society'. The need to acquire certain kinds (and not other kinds) of material objects is a social creation of capitalist civilization. Its broad underpinnings are assured by a range of other institutions. On this foundation, given sets of producers can develop arguments to persuade large groups of purchasers to buy specific kinds of products. This is no doubt a key element in the ability to establish relative monopolies.

Custom also works in still other, subtler ways. There have been established wide linguistic and cultural channels that ensure the greater likelihood that given economic groups will tend to deal with given other ones rather than with those with whom market rationality alone would dictate. Real economic transactions in the capitalist world-economy have depended to a greater extent than we admit on links of community and family, familiarity and trust. And while, up to a point, this reduces transaction costs and therefore is rational in market terms, that point has been readily and regularly exceeded, pushing towards a 'customary' monopolizing of production not determined by market considerations.

Competition, we have said, always comes along to undermine the monopolies. But in order to do so, competitors also cannot rely simply on the market, for the market has been rigged against competition by states and by custom. Potential competitors must usually act first to change the states and to change custom. They have done this by using one set of states against another, or by creating political coalitions within states to change state policy, or by acting in the social arena to change the social definitions of customary and expected behavior, in part by changing immediate taste preferences, in part by attacking more fundamental value premises.

Thus, the politics of accumulation has been a constant battle, which has led to the sapping of the monopolies that have ensured overall expansion of the world-economy; this regular sapping of monopolies, however slow it is, this repeatedly increased degree of competition, has led to the profit squeezes and long stagnations we call Kondratieff B-phases. Each time there is such a stagnation, the system is out of equilibrium. To permit the system to resume its expansion and therefore its ability to ensure the endless accumulation of capital, some adjustments must be made.

Three standard kinds of adjustments are possible, all of which serve to augment overall levels of profit, and therefore to provide the basis of renewed expansion of the world-economy. One can seek to lower the cost of producing competitive products. One can seek to find new buyers for competitive products. One can find new products to produce which will be relatively monopolized yet have a significant market. All three of these adjustments have been made each time there has been a global profit squeeze.

One way to lower the costs of production is to reduce the cost of inputs. But while this may increase profits for one producer, it may lower them for another. Globally, it may change little. The more effective way to lower costs of production is to lower the costs of labour—by further mechanization, by changing law or custom causing lower real wages, or by geographical displacement of production to zones of lower labour costs. These tactics work; they do reduce the cost of labour.

However, these tactics contradict the other mode of increasing profits, if not profit rates, which is that of increasing effective demand. In order to increase effective demand, the global absolute level of reward for labour input must go up, not down. How can these two needs be reconciled? Historically, there has been only one way—by geographical disjuncture. Whenever, in more favoured regions of the world-system, political steps are taken to raise in some way effective demand (increases in wage levels, and in the social wage or state-controlled redistribution), steps have been taken in other parts of the world-system to increase the number of producers at low wage levels. The latter has taken two main forms: transforming rural, land-based workers into more urban, part lifetime wage workers; and expanding the boundaries of the world-economy to include in the world's work force peoples who have previously been rural producers, often largely subsistence producers.

The third and most publicized way to restore profit levels has been of course through technological change, that is, the creation of new so-called leading products which can serve as the locus of monopolized, high-profit operations. This too requires considerable state intervention and reconstruction of 'custom' to ensure monopolization. Without this, the efforts of imaginative entrepreneurs are likely to be stillborn.

In this model of the dilemma of accumulation, the repeated pattern of monopolization, leading to profit squeeze because of increased competition, and the restoration of profit levels (and thus of equilibrium) by counter-action, wherein do we find constraints on the possibility that effective adjustments can indefinitely be made? These constraints probably do not lie in the arena of continued technological inventiveness, although these new products may be moving towards exhausting the ecological balance of the biosphere. They are more likely to be found in the arena of increasing effective demand, since this requires political action that in the long run undermines profitability in other ways. This will be the next dilemma we discuss.

It is in the first mechanism of adjustment, enlarging the low cost sector of the wage force, that we find the strongest constraint of the three, since there are two inherent limits in this process: new zones to include in the world-economy, a limit we seem already to have reached; exhaustion of the reserve of rural, land-based labour to pull in as urban part lifetime wage workers, a limit we will approach in the near future. Can we substitute a reserve army of urban marginals (a very fast-growing segment of the world's population) for that of rural land-based workers? Perhaps, but urban marginals are a far greater threat to the legitimization of states than rural land-based workers.

It is clear that the dilemmas of accumulation lead us directly into the dilemmas of legitimization of political institutions, perhaps a still greater Achilles heel of capitalist civilization.

The Dilemma of Political Legitimization

The dilemma of legitimization of capitalist civilization is straightforward. All historical systems survive by rewarding the cadres of the system. All known historical systems have also had to hold in line large masses of the population who are materially and socially ill-rewarded. The usual way to do the latter has been a combination of force and faith—faith in the sanctity of rulers combined with belief in the inevitability of hierarchy.

For several centuries (roughly between the late fifteenth and the end of eighteenth centuries), capitalist civilization thought it could utilize the ancient mode of legitimation. This was the period of the construction of the central states primarily via absolutist monarchs, as well as the construction of the interstate system. It was the period of creating the winners, and establishing a hierarchy of states within the interstate system. The cadres of the system were offered rewards for entering into close linkage to the winning state structures. We have already seen how important it has always been for entrepreneurs to have the support of strong state structures. These states did receive the support of the cadres.

However, capitalist civilization, as has been repeatedly analysed for 150 years now, was undermining those belief systems that assured the relative acquiescence of the mass of the population. The combination of scientism (linked to the requirements of technological innovation), bureaucratization of the state structures (required for the efficiency of the accumulation process), and the systematic mobility of large populations (required by the evolving work force needs of capitalist productive activity) required a massive renovation of political culture. It was the French Revolution that served as the catalyst of this renovation. Its impact was to make the concept of popular sovereignty the new moral justification for the political system of historical capitalism.

The dilemma then became how to continue to reward the cadres while somehow ensuring the loyalty of the large majority of the population who had become the theoretical depository of legitimacy. In the nineteenth century, this dilemma was posed as the problem of how to incorporate the working classes as well as the cadres into the state structures of the core states of the capitalist world-economy, which at the time were located primarily in western Europe and North America. It constituted a dilemma in that, given the level of absolute surplus-value at the time, if the reward for the working classes were too high, the reward for the cadres would be seriously affected. This was the so-called class struggle, a struggle that was in fact successfully contained historically.

The mode of reconciling the promise of ever-increasing rewards for the cadres and the demands of the working classes for a *quid pro quo* for their loyalty to the state was to offer the latter a small piece of the pie. What was offered was not enough to threaten the accumulation of capital—indeed it perhaps even enlarged it through the expansion of world effective demand—but this offer was combined with hope that this small part of the pie would expand over time along with the expansion of capital accumulation.

The solution was made of adjustment that solved the problem in the short term but reinforced it in the long term, as it created a continual pressure to realize the hope by increasing the share of the working classes. During the nineteenth century, nonetheless, the adjustment mechanism worked remarkably well. Over that period, the working classes of the core countries were offered two paths of increased reward: the path of political participation in elections, or the slow but continuous expansion of the suffrage; and the path of state-imposed redistribution, or the slow but continuous expansion of social legislation and the social wage or welfare state. Along with this went socially guaranteed hope, incarnated not merely in the dominant ideology of liberalism but in the supposedly alternative ideology of socialism.

By 1914, we saw the results—working classes in the core countries well integrated into their respective states, having become both patriotic and reformist. This solution did not in fact impede the ability of the cadres to expand significantly their own incomes, because the solution took place within a framework of massive expansion of total worldwide accumulation, and the significantly increased exploitation of what we today call the South.

The First World War weakened the political hold of the core states on the South. The political integration of their populations now became critical for the stable functioning of the world-system. The dilemma of political legitimization, played out in the nineteenth century within the core states, was replicated for the whole world in the twentieth century. The question was still how to offer the cadres ever-increased reward but also to offer the masses (now of the whole world) a small part of the pie and reformist hope. This solution was what we call Wilsonianism, which offered to repeat on a world scale what had been done within the core states previously. Wilsonianism offered an analogy to the suffrage in national self-determination (the political parity of all states within interstate structures parallel to the political parity of all citizens within a state). And Wilsonianism also offered an analogy to social legislation and the welfare state in the concept of the economic development of underdeveloped nations assisted by development aid (or the welfare state on a world level).

This adjustment seemed at first to work as well, culminating in the political decolonizations and the coming to power in the 1945–65 period of national liberation movement throughout the Third World. Unlike the adjustments of the nineteenth century, however, the adjustments of the twentieth century were not, and could not be, underwritten by a further geographical expansion of the capitalist world-economy. Therefore, the limits of what could be offered in world redistribution without having a serious negative impact on the share of surplus value accorded to the cadres of the system were reached circa 1970. Since that time, Wilsoniamism has been in retreat. The very normal downturn of the world-economy, the world economic stagnation we have been in since then, has seen all the usual processes of adjustment discussed previously in terms of the dilemma of accumulation. But the capacities of the world-system to make the adjustments necessary to maintain the legitimization of the nation-states has shown acute signs of strain.

We have therefore seen, as a growing process in the 1970s and 1980s, the political collapse of the erstwhile national liberation movements in the South, of the Communist parties in what used to be the socialist bloc, and even of Keynesianism/social-democracy in the core states. These collapses have been the result of the withdrawal of mass support for these movements which had previously, after a century of struggle, actually come to political power. But this withdrawal of popular support marked also the abandonment of reformist hope. It thereby removed one of the binding forces of the system of states, and removed in effect their popular legitimization. If, however, the states are no longer legitimized, they cannot contain the political struggles. From the point of view of the capitalist world-system, this collapse of left strategy has been a disaster, since far from being revolutionary the classical left strategy has served as part of the integrating glue of capitalist civilization.

The Dilemma of the Geocultural Agenda

Capitalist civilization has also been built around a geocultural theme which has never previously been dominant: the centrality of the individual as the so-called subject of history. Individualism presents a dilemma, because it is a double-edged sword. On the one hand, by placing the emphasis on individual initiative, capitalist civilization has harnessed self-interest both to the flourishing and to the maintenance of the system. The Promethean myth has encouraged, rewarded, and legitimated the effort of individuals—

not merely entrepreneurs, but the working classes as well—to maximize efficiency and to release the power of human imagination. Indeed, the Promethean myth has done still more, for which it is seldom given credit. It is also responsible for the invention of the concept of formal political organizations of individuals, including the creation and vast expansion paradoxically of the anti-systemic movements themselves. Thus, even anti-individualist social consciousness has been predicated on the summation of individual energies and on individual faith in the efficaciousness of such social action. And, as we have seen, the result has been socially constructed hope, which in turn has served as a key preservative of the world-system.

There is, however, another face to individualism, which is why there is a dilemma of the geocultural agenda. For individualism encourages the race of all against all in a particularly virulent form, since it legitimizes this race not for a small elite alone but for the entirety of mankind. Furthermore, it is logically limitless. Indeed, a good deal of philosophical and social science discourse of modern times has centred on the collective and individual dangers of this social release of unalloyed self-seeking.

The problem for capitalist civilization, from the outset, has been how to reconcile the positive and negative consequences of having established the individual as the subject of history. Conservative ideologists have of course always warned of impending disaster, as have socialist theorists, although in practice neither the conservative nor the socialist ideologists (nor the movements they have inspired) have been willing for very long to struggle directly against this geocultural agenda. Rather, they have accommodated themselves to it and sought to turn it towards their own ends.

By what mechanisms then has the contradiction been contained? It has been contained by emphasizing simultaneously two opposite themes, pursuing them simultaneously, and zigzagging between them. The two emphases, or practices, have been universalism on the one hand and racism-sexism on the other. They are both quintessential products of capitalist civilization. They are seeming opposites, but in fact quite complementary. It is in the strange and precarious link between the two that capitalist civilization has contained the dilemma of the geocultual agenda of the individual as the subject of history.

What is the praxis of universalism? It involves theoretically the moral homogenization of mankind. It is not only the assertion that all persons are endowed with the same human rights but also the assertion that there are universals of human behaviour we can ascertain and analyse. Therefore, universalism tends to view askance any and all incrustation either of human privilege or of the claim that some groups inherently perform better than others.

The praxis of racism and sexism is exactly the opposite. It is the assertion that all persons are not endowed with the same human rights, but are rather arrayed in a biologically or culturally definitive hierarchy. This hierarchy determines their rights and privileges, and their place in the collective work process. It is explained and justified by the fact that some groups inherently perform differently from (and better than) others.

The most extraordinary fact of capitalist civilization over 500 years is that the intensity of belief in these two themes, and the degree to which they have been implemented in social practice, have grown side by side, in tandem. It has been as though any increase in the one praxis brought forth the increase in the other. If we return to the two faces of individualism—individualism as the spur of energy, initiative, and imagination; and individualism as the limitless struggle of all against all—it can be seen how the two practices (universalism and racism-sexism) emerge from and limit the extent of the disequilibrating impact of the contradiction involved in the geocultural agenda.

On the one hand, universalism leads to the conclusion that the contradiction is not real, since the limitless struggle is in fact the spur to initiative, and therefore any privilege that emerges is justified as the consequence of superior performance in a situation where all have equal opportunity to try. This argument has been codified in the twentieth century as meritocracy, in which those on top in the process of capitalist accumulation have merited their position.

On the other hand, racism-sexism becomes the explanation of why those on the bottom have gotten there. They have shown less initiative, even when the possibility has been offered them. They have lost out in the limitless struggle of all against all because they are inherently (if not biologically, then at least culturally) incapable of doing better. To return to our discussion of the balance sheet, universalism becomes the explanation and justification of the improved balance sheet for the minority, and racism-sexism becomes the explanation and justification of the worse balance sheet for the majority.

The way in which these two practices contain each other is that it has always been possible to use the one against the other: to use racism-sexism to prevent universalism from moving too far in the direction of egalitarianism; to use universalism to prevent racism-sexism from moving too far in the direction of a caste system that would inhibit the work force mobility so necessary for the capitalist accumulation process. This is what we mean by the zigzag process.

The constraint on this zigzag comes from the escalation of demands upon the states combined with the inherent impossibility of meeting them—the strained dilemma of accumulation leading to to the strained dilemma of political legitimation. As a result, there have been ever greater demands to realize the egalitarian potential of universalism combined with ever greater demands to realize the inegalitarian caste-like potential of racism and sexism.

What has begun to happen is that the two practices, far from containing each other, are making each other fly further and further apart. We see this in the debates that have come to the surface about the cultural content of our educational systems, one of the central purveyors of the geocultural agenda. If the schools are to be universalist, is this the universalism of one particular group, the world upper stratum? But if they are to be 'multi-cultural', are we not promoting the cultural disunity the educational system is theoretically designed to overcome? If the individual is the subject of history, should we not provide access via individual merit? But if the individual is the subject of history, must we not restore to individuals from the lower strata the opportunities of which they have been socially deprived in order to perform objectively well? This debate is increasingly a dialogue of the deaf, in which however both sides are increasingly mobilized, politically and culturally.

Crisis of the Historical System

Let us put the three pieces together. Capitalist civilization has been elaborated within contradictions. This is not unusual; all historical systems have contradictions. In the case of historical capitalism, there are three principal contradictions, which I have tried to describe briefly. Each contradiction has been historically contained by adjustment mechanisms. But in each case these adjustment mechanisms have become strained. We may say that the cumulation of these strains means that the modern world-system as such is approaching, is probably already in, a systemic crisis.

A systemic crisis may be described as a situation in which the system has reached a bifurcation point, or the first of successive bifurcation points. When systems come to be far from points of equilibrium, they reach bifurcation points, wherein multiple, as opposed to unique, solutions to instability become possible. The system has at that point what we may think of as choice between possibilities. The choice depends both on the history of the system and the immediate strength of elements external to the internal logic of the system. These external elements are what we call 'noise' in terms of the system. When systems are functioning normally, 'noise' is ignored. But in situations far from equilibrium, the random variations in the 'noise' have a magnified effect because of the high increase in the disequilibrium. Thereupon, the system, now acting chaotically, will reconstruct itself quite radically in ways that are internally unpredictable, but which lead nonetheless to new forms of order. There can be, there usually is, under such conditions, not one but a cascade of bifurcations until a new system, that is, a new structure of long-term relative equilibrium, is established and once again we find ourselves in a situation of deterministic stability. The new emergent system is probably more complex; it is in any case different from the old system.

If we apply this general schema which applies to all systems— from physico-chemical to biological to social systems—to our immediate concern, i.e., the future prospects of capitalist civilization, we can summarize the situation as follows. The capitalist world-economy is a historical system that has been relatively stable, that is, operating within the logic of certain rules for some 500 years now. We have tried to evaluate its balance sheet, and then to indicate the strains on the processes of adjustment necessary to maintain its equilibrium. We have suggested the reasons why it is reaching or has reached bifurcation points. We seem to be in the midst of a process of cascading bifurcations that may last some 50 more years. We can be sure some new historical order will emerge. We cannot be sure what that order will be.

Concretely, we may symbolize the first bifurcation as the effect of the world revolution of 1968 which continued up to and including the so-called collapse of the communisms in 1989, the second bifurcation. In the multiple local expressions of the world revolution of 1968 we had the expression, of course, of a rebellion against capitalist civilization and its immediate main supporting structure, US hegemony in the world-system, with which the USSR was seen as being in collusion. But we also had a rejection of all the old anti-systemic movements—social-democrats in the West, the Communist parties in the socialist bloc, the national liberation movements in the Third World—as ineffective failures, and worse still, as tacit legitimators of the existing world-system.

For the revolutionaries of 1968, there was an equation of reformism, Enlightenment values, and the faith in state structures as political instruments of change. They opposed all three. The countercultural clothes of the 1968 revolutionaries were not so much an affirmation of individualism in general (as is often said) as they were a specific affirmation of one of the thrusts (that towards individual fulfilment) and a specific rejection of the contradictory thrust (that towards egotistic consumerism).

The events of 1968 around the world followed the typical form of initial bifurcations. The swings in social sentiment were extremely strong. The events were a rupture, breaking for the first time in a significant way the widespread legitimation of state structures as such, which had been such a stabilizing force in capitalist civilization. Of course, the immediate demands of the 1968 revolutionaries were in part met by adjustments of state social policy, in part suppressed by the authorities. The adjustments were more frequent in the core zones of the capitalist world-economy than in the periphery. They were least made in the socialist countries. On the contrary, Brezhnevian stagnation was specifically suppressive of 1968 demands. The reason why fewer adjustments were made in the peripheral zones was that the world accumulation process left them with less flexibility. Their state structures all suffered severe financial squeezes in the Kondratieff B-phase, and were in no position to buy off protest. Furthermore, these governments in power were by and large precisely those of the anti-systemic movements, which meant the pressure on government policy such movements would normally make was absent.

One by one, these governments came undone, and were forced into IMF tutelage (and national illegitimacy) by the careening oil prices, the debt imbroglio, and falling terms of trade. The last of these governments to fall were the Communist regimes of eastern Europe, which have now gone the way of other Third World countries. The second in the cascade of bifurcations is thus symbolized by 1989. Seemingly quite different from 1968, it actually pursued parallel themes: disillusionment with the possibility of a state-led reformist path to equality in the world-system.

This collapse of the Communisms was an even bigger blow to the stability of capitalist civilization than the 1968 events. Previously some would excuse the failures of some anti-systemic movements by suggesting that they had been insufficiently on the Soviet model, and therefore inherently weak. But when even the Soviet model collapsed, and from disillusionment within, the possibility of progressive steady social change seemed to become very remote. The loss of hope in Leninism has really been the loss of hope in centrist liberalism. The ex-Communist countries have simply become reintegrated in terms of perception into the category of non-core zones of the world-system. The particularity of this second bifurcation was that it brought in its train the disintegration of state structures without the optimistic (and stabilizing) effect of the post-1918 and post-1945 nationalist decolonizations. The Wilsonian call for self-determination has not yet lost all its power perhaps, but it has definitely lost its bloom.

Where then is capitalist civilization moving? On the one hand, the capitalist world-economy will move steadily forward on its well-worn ruts—the recreation of major poles of accumulation, Japan (probably in collaboration with the UD) on the one hand, and (western) Europe on the other. Between them, in the early twenty-first century, we should see a new major expansion of world production based on new monopolized production sectors. However, because of the contraction of the pool of world reserve labour, it is not sure that they will be able to maintain the same high rate of accumulation as heretofore.

With this expansion will come necessarily a further polarization of reward and of social structures. We have already argued why this is putting an impossible strain on political legitimation. We are thus moving into a time of massive local, regional, and world disorders, a time of troubles, which will be far less structured (and therefore far less contained) than the German-US world wars of the twentieth century and the wars of national liberation that came in their wake.

The strain on political legitimation, the inability to contain that dilemma, is leading to the disintegration of the faith in progress that contained the dilemma of the geocultural agenda. Since people no longer believe that the omnipotent individual is indeed the subject of history, they have been searching for the protection of groups. The new geocultural theme has already been proclaimed: it is the theme of identity, identity as encrusted in a very elusive concept called 'culture', or to be more exact in 'cultures'. But this new theme simply creates a new dilemma of the geocultural agenda. On the one hand, the call for multiple identities is a call for the equality of all 'cultures'. On the other hand, it is a call for the particularity, and therefore the tacit hierarchy, of all 'cultures'. As people move between the two contradictory thrusts, there will be the constant redefinition of the boundaries of the groups that have these 'cultures'. But the very concept of 'culture' is based on the assumed stability of these boundaries.

We may therefore expect explosions in all directions. Those whose 'cultures' seem to be excluded from current privilege will turn to the three kinds of political mechanisms that can offer political exit from the inequality of the groups. One mechanism is the cultivation of radical alterity. A second mechanism is the constitution of larger units with effective armed power. The third is individual transgression of the cultural boundaries, escape by upward individual 'cultural' ascent. None of these mechanisms is new, but all were previously subordinated to the state-oriented reformist/pseudo-revolutionary searches for state power as the road to transformation. The collective power of individuals is now being replaced by the particular power of collectivities.

In the twenty-five to fifty years to come, we are likely to see different forms of disorder in the South and in the North. In the South, there will probably be no more of the national liberation movements that have dominated the landscape throughout the twentieth century. They have played their historical role, for good or ill. Few believe they have a further role to play. Instead we will see the three options that have come to prominence in the last two decades. I shall call them the Khomeini option, the Saddam Hussein option, and the 'boat people' option. In terms of the equilibrium of capitalist civilization, each is equally unsettling.

The Khomeini option is the option of radical alterity, of total collective refusal to play by the rules of the world-system. When engaged in by a large enough group with enough collective resources, it can provide a formidable challenge to systemic equilibrium. A single instance of it may perhaps be tamed, if only with great difficulty. But multiple simultaneous explosions would wreak havoc.

The Saddam Hussein option is quite different but equally difficult to handle. It is the path of investment in the creation of larger states that are heavily militarized with the intent of engaging in actual warfare with the North. It is not an easy option to pursue and it may seem possible, after the Gulf war, for the North to stand up to it comfortably. Let us not be deceived by appearances. As this option becomes the policy of more and more states, it will be increasingly difficult to counter it easily. As it is, let us not fail to notice that total military defeat was insufficient to end permanently a Saddam Hussein option even in Iraq.

Finally there is the 'boat people' option, the massive, relentless drive of households to migrate illegally to wealthier climes, to escape from the South to the North. Boat people can be sent back, but with difficulty; and more will keep coming. Over the coming twenty-five to fifty years, we may expect enormous numbers to succeed in this South-North migration. The double reality of the material conditions gap and the demographic gap makes it highly improbable that any state policy in the North can be seriously effective in stemming the flow.

What then will happen in the economically still buoyant North? Recall that we are predicating a decline in the efficiency of state structures, even in the North. The phenomenon of the 'Third World within' in the core zones of the capitalist world-economy will become massive as the demographic balance shifts. North America has the largest south contingent today. Western Europe is catching up. The phenomenon is beginning even in Japan, which has erected the strongest legal and cultural barriers of any state in the North.

The demographic transformation, caused by weakening state structures, will in turn weaken them further. Social disorder will once again become normal in the core zones. In the last twenty years there has been much discussion on this under the false label of increased crime. What we shall be seeing is increased civil warfare. This is the face of the time of troubles. The scramble for protection has already begun. The states cannot provide it. For one thing they do not have the money; for another they do not have the legitimation. We shall see instead the expansion of private protection armies and police structures—by the multiple cultural groups, by the corporate production structures, by local communities, by religious bodies, and of course by crime syndicates. This should not be termed anarchism; it is rather deterministic chaos.

Where shall we come out? For out of chaos comes new order. We cannot know for certain, except for one thing. Capitalist civilization will be over; its particular historical system will be no more. The most we can say beyond that is to outline a few alternative possible historical trajectories—outline them, that is, in broad brush strokes without the institutional detail that is entirely unforeseeable.

Three types of social formulae seem plausible in the light of the history of the world-system. One is a sort of neo-feudalism that would reproduce in a far more equilibrated form the developments of the time of troubles—a world of parcellized sovereignties, of considerably more autarkic regions, of local hierarchies. This might be made compatible with maintaining (but probably not furthering) the current relatively high level of technology. Endless accumulation of capital could no longer function as the mainspring of such a system, but it would certainly be an inegalitarian system. What would legitimate it? Perhaps a return to a belief in natural hierarchies.

A second formula might be a sort of democratic fascism. Such a formula would involve a caste-like division of the world into two strata, the top one incorporating perhaps a fifth of the world's population. Within this stratum, there could be a high degree of egalitarian distribution. On the basis of such a community of interests within such a large group, they might have the strength to keep the other 80 per cent in the position of a totally disarmed working proletariat. Hitler's new world order had such a vision in mind. It failed, but then it defined itself in terms of too narrow a top stratum.

A third formula might be a still more radical worldwide highly decentralized, highly egalitarian world order. This seems the most utopian of the three but it is scarcely to be ruled out. This kind of world order has been foreshadowed in much intellectual musings of the past centuries. The increased political sophistication and technological expertise we now have makes it doable, but not at all certain. It would require accepting certain real limitations in consumption expenditures. But it does not mean merely a socialization of poverty, for then it would be politically impossible to realize.

Are there still other possibilities? Of course there are. What is important to recognize is that all three historical options are really there, and the choice will depend on our collective world behaviour over the next fifty years. Whichever option is chosen, it will not be the end of history, but in a real sense its beginning. The human social world is still very young in cosmological time.

In 2050 or 2100, when we look back at capitalist civilization, what will we think? We will possibly be quite unfair. Whichever option we choose for a new system, we may feel it necessary to denigrate the one just past, that of capitalist civilization. We will emphasize its evils and ignore whatever it did achieve. By the year 3000, we may remember it as a fascinating exercise in human history—either an exceptional and aberrant period, but just possibly a historically important moment of very long transition to a more egalitarian world; or an inherently unstable form of human exploitation after which the world returned to more stable forms. *Sic transit gloria!*